D1015412

Being a genuine Kringel, I believe my endorsement carries some weight on Christmas. As a pastor, I am always looking for new ways to present fresh looks at key holiday moments. *40 Days of Christmas* presents one day after another of life-giving thoughts and takeaways. Pastors will want this book as a resource for messages but also for personal reflection.

—KEVIN KRINGEL, *lead pastor, Life Church, Roscoe, Illinois and author of* Relevant Acts

*40 Days of Christmas* is outstanding! I look forward to rereading it with my family during the Christmas season. Both meaningful and inspiring, this book truly captures the essence of what Christmas is all about. The eye-opening message will challenge you, and the daily prayers will encourage and strengthen your faith. This devotional will take you deeper in your personal relationship with Christ as you discover the true spirit of Christmas.

—BILLY WELCH, *lead pastor, North Pole Assembly of God, North Pole, Alaska*

*40 Days of Christmas* is a real gem! As a one-day celebration, Christmas seems to pass all too quickly. We rarely take the time to adequately reflect on its meaning. Castleberry's book uses the forty days of Christmas to offer us a powerful alternative. Start each of these forty days reading a biblical text followed by a Christmas devotion and a prayer. Every devotion will open your heart and enlighten your mind. So many interesting insights to ponder. Believe me, you'll treasure this book and want to share it with others!

—FRANK D. MACCHIA, *D. Theol., D.D., theologian,*
*Vanguard University of Southern California*
*and Bangor University, Wales (UK)*

*40 Days of Christmas* makes the familiar story of Christmas come alive for its readers. It is filled with fresh insights, new perspectives, profound theology, and helpful observations. I've preached about Christmas for twenty years, and I learned something new on almost every page that deepened my love for and understanding of Christmas. Staying close to the text, Castleberry offers helpful observations on everything from Christmas trees, Christmas music, Santa Claus, and the liturgical calendar, and uses it all to add depth, meaning, and a heartfelt connection to the Christmas story. *40 Days of Christmas* offers reflections that are new, interesting, and right. This will change how you go through the Christmas season.

—SCOTT DUDLEY, *senior pastor,*
*Bellevue Presbyterian Church, Bellevue, Washington*

This devotional takes the reader through Scripture, adding stories and thoughts that point the way to Jesus Christ. The tone of the devotional is so inviting. It's as if you are having a conversation over a cup of coffee about the things that matter to God. Well written for the forty days of Advent, this devotional will be picked up each season of every year.

—SHIRLEY V. HOOGSTRA, *president,*
*Council for Christian Colleges & Universities*

Rarely can you read something in two minutes that changes the way you see something you have been familiar with your entire life. If you give two minutes of your time for the next forty days to read this book, you will see Christmas in a different way—from the tree that is in your living room to the sentiment that is in your heart. Dr. Castleberry is a genius, and he translates his intelligence in such a way that people like me can get it. It is fun to read something that makes you a better person. Merry Christmas and happy new life!

—DEAN CURRY, *pastor, Life Center,*
*Tacoma, Washington*

*40 Days of Christmas* is a wonderfully accessible and transforming journey through the Christmas season, an edifying and inspiring blend of theological depth coupled with the simplicity and purity of devotion to Christ. A wonderful gift for friends, family, and especially those who may have lost sight of the real meaning of Christmas.

—GRANT GOODEVE, *actor,*
*singer, songwriter*

The pages of *40 Days of Christmas* are filled with profound insights! Reading these reflections is sure to help you approach the celebration of Christ's birth with fresh joy and faith-filled anticipation.

—JOHN LINDELL, *lead pastor, James River Church,*
*Ozark, Missouri*

Dr. Joseph Castleberry has unlocked the spirit of Christmas with this timely new book. For those seeking to reflect on the true meaning of the Advent season, this book is for you.

—A. J. RICE, *CEO of Publius PR, Washington, DC*

*40 Days of Christmas* provides a refreshing and inspirational look at Christmas. After reading it, I'm motivated more than ever to live the spirit of Christmas throughout the entire year.

—CHAPLAIN (COLONEL) SCOTT MCCHRYSTAL,
*US Army (retired)*

# 40
## DAYS
## OF
## CHRISTMAS

# 40 DAYS OF CHRISTMAS

*Celebrating the Glory of Our Savior*

JOSEPH CASTLEBERRY

**BroadStreet**
PUBLISHING

BroadStreet Publishing® Group, LLC
Savage, Minnesota, USA
BroadStreetPublishing.com

40 Days of Christmas:
*Celebrating the Glory of Our Savior*

Copyright © 2018 Joseph Castleberry

978-1-4245-5757-8 (hardcover)
978-1-4245-5758-5 (e-book)

All rights reserved. No part of this book may be reproduced in any form, except for brief quotations in printed reviews, without permission in writing from the publisher.

Unless otherwise noted, all Scripture quotations are taken from the Holy Bible, New International Version®, NIV® Copyright ©1973, 1978, 1984, 2011 by Biblica, Inc.® Used by permission. Scripture quotations marked NLT are taken from the Holy Bible, New Living Translation, copyright © 1996, 2004, 2007 by Tyndale House Foundation. Used by permission of Tyndale House Publishers, Inc., Carol Stream, Illinois 60188, USA. All rights reserved. Scripture marked KJV is taken from the King James Version of the Bible. Scripture quotations marked NKJV are taken from the New King James Version®. Copyright © 1982 by Thomas Nelson. Used by permission. All rights reserved. Scripture quotations marked ESV are taken from the Holy Bible, English Standard Version. ESV® Text Edition: 2016. Copyright © 2001 by Crossway Bibles, a publishing ministry of Good News Publishers. Other Scripture quotations are those of the author.

Stock or custom editions of BroadStreet Publishing titles may be purchased in bulk for educational, business, ministry, fundraising, or sales promotional use. For information, please email info@broadstreetpublishing.com.

Cover design by Chris Garborg at garborgdesign.com
Interior design and typesetting by Katherine Lloyd at theDESKonline.com

Printed in China
18 19 20 21 22 5 4 3 2 1

To J. Calvin Holsinger, PhD,
a dear friend full of years, who went to be
with the Lord during Advent on December 15,
the day I began to write this book.

And to my granddaughter Miranda Hope Austin,
whose vigorous advent into this world
occurred on the same day in my home.

# Contents

# WHY FORTY DAYS?

*a* friend recently wrote on one of my social media sites, "It's January 2, and I'm so excited to throw out our Christmas tree!" I immediately responded, "You aren't doing Christmas right if you quit before Epiphany!" Unfortunately, many people do not get the most out of their Christmas celebration. They let the hustle and bustle and kitsch ruin the whole thing. They start moaning when their city or town puts up the Christmas lights before Thanksgiving Day and then wonder why seasonal affective disorder has them in its clutches by December 26. I have never heard a child say, "I can't wait until Christmas is over!" How sad it feels to hear an adult say it. What a waste!

Long ago, the founders of our culture designed Christmas in December with the desire to lift the spirits of our people during the darkest time of the year. Celebrating Christmas the right way offers a number of wonderful benefits that will improve our mental state, delight our families, strengthen our economy, and contribute to our spiritual growth and well-being. Its design motivates us to save money throughout the year. It provides a season to love our family and friends tangibly with cards and phone calls and presence and presents. It leads us to cultivate a childlike attitude with corresponding childlike joy. It gives us an excuse to set aside fasting (diets) and eat a great feast. Most importantly, it stimulates us to think about God's love for humankind and to meditate on the beauty and glory of the birth of our Savior. It offers many other benefits as well.

One of the worst feelings in the world is getting nothing for Christmas, and getting nothing out of it feels just as bad. You need to read this book so you can get the most out of Christmas!

I like to celebrate Christmas for a full forty days. Forty days is a biblically significant time period, often associated with fasting or trial—such as the time Jesus spent fasting under temptation in the wilderness. Many people only celebrate Christmas for a day or two, and some Christians do not celebrate it at all, seeing it as a pagan convention. But wiser generations before us divided the holiday into three seasons on the church calendar to prepare for Christmas (Advent), celebrate it (Christmastime), and live it out (Epiphany).

Because the Sundays of Advent always occur on different dates, I have chosen to frame the calendar of these Christmas reflections across the seasons of Advent, Christmas, and Epiphany, beginning on November 28, the first possible Sunday of Advent. I have chosen to recognize a few feast days dedicated to biblical personages on the historic church calendar. On each day I have offered a Bible reading, a reflection on the text or exposition of it, and a prayer, with hopes of adding information, creativity, and spiritual depth to each day of this special period of fuss and feasting, helping you enrich your celebration of Christmas.

I feel compelled to confess that not all of these reflections are, strictly speaking, Bible studies. Sometimes the featured Bible verse provides only a starting place for the reflection that follows. I hope I have not arrived at any unbiblical musings, even if some do not conform strictly to the contextual readings of the text provided.

Most of all, I hope that these reflections will help you get the greatest possible joy from this Christmas season. I want to get you started thinking and praying more deeply about this blessed season! I pray that God will speak to you in ways that go far beyond what I have written. Merry Christmas!

*November 28*

# MUSIC
## AT CHRISTMAS

Suddenly a great company of the heavenly host
appeared with the angel, praising God and saying,
"Glory to God in the highest heaven, and on earth
peace to those on whom his favor rests."
—*Luke 2:13–14*

Christmas and music are inseparable. We all know
that the angel chorus sang the announcement of the
birth of the Messiah to Galilean shepherds, even though
the biblical text does not say that they sang. Similarly, in
the New International Version, Mary's *Magnificat* in Luke
1:46 carries the translator's heading "Mary's Song," while
Zechariah's response to the promised Messiah in Luke
1:67 is labeled as "Zechariah's Song." In neither case does
the original text specify that they sang, but their utter-
ances came in the form of lyrical poetry that matches the
genre of first-century hymns. Simeon also bursts out in

poetic praise in Luke 2:29 as Mary and Joseph present the baby Jesus in the temple in Jerusalem. Still, the biblical text never explicitly mentions music or singing in connection to the nativity and infancy of the Messiah.

It doesn't need to. From our own reception of the Christmas tidings, we know instinctively that they sang. We ourselves want to burst out singing when we think of Christmas. In musical theatre, the dialogue moves along in prose, but there are high moments when the play has to break out in song. Likewise, the human story puttered along in prose for centuries awaiting the begetting of God's Son, our Savior, but when the baby came, singing had to break out. In our own lives, we dragged through years of lost wandering in prose until the good news broke into our hearts and set them singing.

*O God, who created the music of the heavenly spheres and gifted humanity with song, receive our praise as we begin singing the songs of Christmas this year. Be blessed as we worship; rejoice over us with singing as we meditate on the meaning of this blessed season. Lift up our hearts through the winter days ahead and let us see Jesus everywhere we go. In the name of him who has made us glad. Amen.*

# O CHRISTMAS TREE

> Then the angel showed me the river of the water
> of life, as clear as crystal, flowing from the throne
> of God and of the Lamb down the middle of the
> great street of the city. On each side of the river
> stood the tree of life, bearing twelve crops of fruit,
> yielding its fruit every month. And the leaves of
> the tree are for the healing of the nations.
> —*Revelation 22:1–2*

*M*any people think of the Christmas tree as a left-over from the pagan winter rituals of Europe, but in fact, the Christmas tree offers a uniquely Christian symbol of deep biblical truths. Undeniably, Europeans have decorated their homes during winter with ever-green boughs from time immemorial, but in the Middle Ages, Christians began setting up "paradise trees" in their homes to commemorate the tree of life on the feast day of Adam and Eve (Christmas Eve).[1] In doing so, they recognized that Jesus came to us as the "second Adam from above," like we intone in "Hark the Herald Angels Sing." The strong biblical significance attached to the new innovation completely surpassed any meaning that puny pagan fir decorations might have had.

As seen in Revelation 22:1–2, the Tree of Life will stand among the redeemed in heaven, but it will have taken on a new ironic meaning. Strangely, when Jewish scholars a few hundred years before the birth of Jesus translated the book of Genesis from Hebrew to Greek in the Septuagint translation that would become the Bible of the early church, they chose an odd word to translate "tree [of life]." Rather than the normal word for a green tree, *dendron* (as in the English word *rhododendron* or "rose tree"), the translators chose *xulon*, which means "a dry stick, a piece of lumber, or dead wood."

As John applied the phrase to heaven, it took on a new meaning. The "tree of life" was not an ordinary tree. It was a dead stick—a piece of lumber that now sprouts leaves that heal the nations and abundantly bears fruit every month of the year. Somehow, a dead stick has become the most powerfully alive tree in the universe. Obviously, the cross of Jesus Christ has become the Tree of Life. The very instrument of Jesus' death has participated in his resurrection, and those who "eat its fruit" will live forever.

Every year, as you decorate your Christmas tree, remember the Tree of Life. When you take it down, remember the dead stick of the cross. Just as your tree went from life to death, you will by faith in Christ ere long pass from death to everlasting life.

*Heavenly Father, please receive our decorated tree and our festive home as an offering of praise and a symbol of longing for our eternal home with you. Let your presence dwell among us richly this season, inspiring us to hope in you, reminding us of the life to come in the world without end, with Christ Jesus our Lord. Amen.*

# THE HOUSE
# OF DAVID

In those days Caesar Augustus issued a
decree that a census should be taken of the entire
Roman world. … And everyone went to their
own town to register. So Joseph also went up
from the town of Nazareth in Galilee to Judea,
to Bethlehem the town of David, because he
belonged to the house and line of David.
—*Luke 2:1, 3–4*

*E*very messianic prophecy finds its origin in David's
plans to build a temple for the worship of Israel's
God. David had inquired of the prophet Nathan as to
whether he should build the Lord a house, and Nathan
jumped to the conclusion that of course he should build
it. But later he returned with a genuine word from God:

"The LORD himself will establish a house for you:
When your days are over and you rest with your

ancestors, I will raise up your offspring to succeed you, your own flesh and blood, and I will establish his kingdom. He is the one who will build a house for my Name, and I will establish the throne of his kingdom forever. I will be his father, and he will be my son." (2 Samuel 7:11–14)

In an initial sense, the prophecy referred to Solomon, but it bore elements he could never truly fulfill. After Solomon's death, the prophets began to look forward to a son of David who would truly reign forever, who would truly be God's Son, who would truly build a house for God. The first Christians saw in Jesus the fulfillment of God's whole Word.

And Jesus still builds a house for God—not a building but a family of sons and daughters. "As many as received Him, to them He gave the right to become children of God, to those who believe in His name" (John 1:12 NKJV). "And we are his house, if indeed we hold firmly to our confidence and the hope in which we glory" (Hebrews 3:6).

The celebration of Christmas goes far beyond the recognition that the Son of God was born of a virgin two thousand years ago. We observe this season of joy because of the billions of sons and daughters who have been born again into the family of God as a result of Jesus' life, death, and resurrection. Jesus has truly built a house for God, and he will reign over that house forever.

*In the name of Jesus, who has brought us salvation unto eternal life, we give thanks to the Father, and to the Holy Spirit, who has drawn us out of darkness into divine light. In this dark season, rule over us. Let your will be done among us as it is in heaven. Amen.*

# A CHILD IS BORN

For to us a child is born, to us a son is given,
and the government will be on his shoulders.
And he will be called Wonderful Counselor,
Mighty God, Everlasting Father, Prince of Peace.
Of the greatness of his government and peace
there will be no end. He will reign on David's
throne and over his kingdom, establishing and
upholding it with justice and righteousness
from that time on and forever.

—*Isaiah 9:6–7*

The prophet Isaiah apparently wrote this splendid royal psalm for use in the coronation of King Hezekiah. Following the practice of ancient Near Eastern courtiers, the Israelites considered the day of a king's coronation his "rebirth" as a child of God. Like a newborn baby receives a name, the newborn King would receive "throne names" and titles, even as we witness to this day with popes and monarchs. The new king of Israel would be known as "Wonderful Counselor, Mighty God, Ever-lasting Father, Prince of Peace."

Old Testament prophecies usually had a near-term meaning that related to the time in which they were given, but the prophecies would carry a "surplus of meaning"—elements that the contemporary fulfillment did not exhaust. In Isaiah's psalm (an example of a psalm outside of the book of Psalms), the surplus of meaning is obvious. No naturally born king was literally a son of God. Neither Hezekiah nor any other king could live up to throne names like "the Mighty God" or "Everlasting Father."

So the psalm points forward to a future Messiah or "anointed one" who would transcend all of his predecessors. While the Davidic kings of old were symbolically sons of God, the Messiah would be the only begotten Son of God. Priests anointed the former kings with oil, but God would pour out the Holy Spirit on the Messiah without measure. The coming Messiah would truly be the Mighty God, the Everlasting Father, the Prince of Peace. And unlike his predecessors, he would truly reign forever.

"O Come, O Come Emmanuel, and ransom captive Israel." The words come from a Christmas carol, but they express the prayers of the Jews for many centuries as they waited for a true king, a true Messiah. On the first Christmas, truly a Child was born unto us, a Son was given, and the government of God will be upon his shoulders.

Jesus has begun his eternal reign, and in the world without end that he will bring, all of God's promises to Israel and to us will find their yes and amen (2 Corinthians 1:20).

*Lord, as you have taught us to pray, may your kingdom come; may your will be done on earth as in heaven. Let your will rule in our lives, in our families, in our churches, in our workplaces, in our leisure, and in our world. This is our greatest desire, for if we seek first your kingdom, all other things will be added to us. Amen.*

*December 2*

# A VIRGIN CONCEIVES

Then Isaiah said, "Hear now, you house of David!
Is it not enough to try the patience of humans?
Will you try the patience of my God also?
Therefore, the Lord himself will give you a sign:
The virgin will conceive and give birth to a son,
and will call him Immanuel. ... Before the
boy knows enough to reject the wrong and
choose the right, the land of the two kings
you dread will be laid waste."
—*Isaiah 7:13–15, 16*

When Isaiah delivered this famous prophecy to King Ahaz of the house of David, the issue at stake involved Judah's security during the Syro-Ephraimite War, in which the kings of Syria and Israel would lay siege to Jerusalem. The prophecy would find initial fulfillment when the *almah* (Hebrew for "young woman" or "virgin") would conceive and bear a child whose name would be Immanuel—"God with us." Careful reading of the context suggests that the young woman in question may have been Isaiah's wife (8:3). The prophecy offered God's help and salvation, but rather than trusting God, the king of Judah appealed to the Assyrian emperor for help. God's prophetic offer was thus frustrated.

But as Isaiah himself declared, no word from God will ever return to him empty, but will accomplish what he desires and achieve the purpose for which he sent it (55:11). A few hundred years later, the Septuagint Bible brought greater sharpness to Isaiah's prophecy. Translators rendered almah as *parthenos* in Greek. While almah can mean virgin, parthenos removes all ambiguity. A chaste, unmarried, young woman who had never had sexual relations with a man would conceive and bear a son. When Matthew announced the fulfillment of Isaiah's prophecy in Jesus, the prophecy unfolded in a clear new meaning that human faithlessness could never frustrate.

The Virgin Mary conceived and bore the very Son of God. Through that miraculous act of new creation, God truly became one of us and dwelt with us in the person of Jesus. His sinless life demonstrated his oneness with the Father, and his powerful words and deeds showed he had received an unprecedented anointing of the Holy Spirit. In his death and resurrection, the Father vindicated his claim to be "God with us." When he comes again to reign, the kingdom of God will defeat every enemy.

Now we need not question whether God's Word will

be frustrated. We should question whether we will do as Ahaz did. Having received God's Word that he will be with us in Christ, will we trust him and receive his salvation, or will we do as Ahaz did and turn to our own devices, seeking a worldly means of help? The true celebration of Christmas requires us to welcome Jesus as our Savior, to believe God's promise, and to trust in God.

*Father, it sometimes seems to us that your promises have failed. Give us faith to trust you more, not less, when our expectations do not seem to be working out. Give us a rock-solid conviction that your sovereignty holds, despite appearances. In you we declare our victory over circumstances. Amen.*

*December 3*

# A FAMILY OF BLESSING

> This is a record of the ancestors of Jesus the
> Messiah, a descendant of David and of Abraham:
> … Judah was the father of Perez … (whose
> mother was Tamar). … Salmon was the father
> of Boaz (whose mother was Rahab). Boaz was
> the father of Obed (whose mother was Ruth). …
> David was the father of Solomon (whose mother
> was Bathsheba, the widow of Uriah). … Jacob was
> the father of Joseph, the husband of Mary. Mary
> gave birth to Jesus, who is called the Messiah.
> —*Matthew 1:1, 3, 5–6, 16 NLT*

Genealogies played an important role for the Jewish people, just as they do for many people today. They tell us where and whom we came from. Through the stories they tell, they preserve a record of our families' values from generation to generation. Matthew's genealogy of Jesus carried precious memories of his family. As children of Abraham, the family of Jesus remembered the destiny they carried to bless all other families of the earth (Genesis 12:3). Like all Jewish people, they confessed that their patriarch Jacob was "a wandering Aramaen" who went to live as a stranger in Egypt (Deuteronomy 26:5). As descendants of migrants, the family of Jesus loved foreigners. The fact that four of the five women mentioned in this genealogy married foreigners—Tamar, Rahab, Ruth, and Bathsheba—proves their affection for them.

Another look at the women in this list reveals that they all suffered from a bad reputation. The Canaanite Tamar had to prostitute herself to Judah in order to get what he owed her. Rahab, also a Canaanite, left a life of prostitution to join the people of God. Ruth, the Moabitess, offered herself to Boaz in a risqué story that could have ended in disaster. The tragedy of Uriah the Hittite still casts a shadow on the character of his wife, Bathsheba. Mary became pregnant in conditions that appeared shameful in her society. One thing remains undeniable: Despite their apparent errors, the family of Jesus—a family preserved by the grace of God—loved these women and remembered them in honor.

Spiritually, all Christians are children of Abraham and members of the family of Christ. Among our family values we still hold dear the love of foreigners and the priority of grace, which has rescued us all from our imperfect reputations. In the birth of the Messiah, salvation has arrived for every family on earth.

*Father of us all, who has both given us life
and adopted us through the new birth, help
us be a blessing to everyone we encounter
this Christmas season. May the message of
salvation that our spiritual ancestors announced,
awaited, and experienced be on our lips in
every "Merry Christmas" we pronounce. May
we find redemption from sin and shame and find
freedom to share our family's love with everyone.
In the name of the Father, and of the Son, and of
the Holy Spirit, amen.*

# HIGHLY FAVORED

In the sixth month of Elizabeth's pregnancy,
God sent the angel Gabriel to Nazareth, a town
in Galilee, to a virgin pledged to be married to a
man named Joseph, a descendant of David. The
virgin's name was Mary. The angel went to her and
said, "Greetings, you who are highly favored!
The Lord is with you."
—*Luke 1:26–28*

At the time of the birth of Jesus, Galilee had many Gentile residents, and people referred to it as Galilee of the Gentiles. Perhaps in contrast to that reality, its population included many very faithful and highly religious Jews. The Gospel of Matthew calls Joseph "a righteous man," a term that indicated that he lived out the law of Moses with great care and that he led a life of prayer and spiritual discipline. It appears that Mary also belonged to the community of the righteous.

Both Mary and Joseph received angelic visitations to announce the plan that God intended for them and for the salvation of the world. God clearly saw them as people who would parent his Son well. At the same time, no human parents could ever have merited such an honor. When the angel greeted Mary, he recognizes her as "begraced" (*kecharitōmenē*), or "full of grace." God's choice credited the godliness of Mary and Joseph, but their election (like ours) depended on the unmerited favor of God.

Among Mary's outstanding character traits, her humility stands out. She humbly submits to God's plan, agreeing to bear God's Son. Her song, the Magnificat, clearly shows that she recognized herself as a lowly person. A proud person could never have borne the shame of a premarital pregnancy and would never have submitted to traveling to Bethlehem while pregnant or to giving birth to her child in a stable. Despite her knowledge of the miraculous nature of her child, she marvels over and over again at the wondrous things he said and did. She proved herself to be a person of truly admirable character.

Still, Mary, like the rest of us, could never have saved herself by her considerable efforts to live a godly life. Salvation has always come by grace—in the Old Testament as well as the New. The grace of Christmas calls us all to adopt the same spirit of humble thankfulness and submission to God that Mary modeled. Like her, we have received high favor—grace upon grace—in receiving the miracle of Christmas.

*Lord Jesus Christ, who has favored us with grace and truth, we pray that we might walk in the humility of those who have received salvation through no merit of their own. In total gratitude, we commit ourselves to pursue godliness as Joseph and Mary did, to seek your will and to do it, not only at Christmas, but every day of our lives. Amen.*

# CHRISTMAS LEADERS

> While [Mary] was still a virgin, she became
> pregnant through the power of the Holy Spirit.
> Joseph, to whom she was engaged, was a righteous
> man and did not want to disgrace her. … As he
> considered this, an angel … appeared to him in
> a dream. "Joseph …" the angel said, "do not be
> afraid to take Mary as your wife. For the child …
> was conceived by the Holy Spirit … You are to
> name him Jesus, for he will save his people from
> their sins." … When Joseph woke up, he did as the
> angel of the Lord commanded. … But he did not
> have sexual relations with [Mary] until her son
> was born. And Joseph named him Jesus.
> —*Matthew 1:18–21, 24–25 NLT*

Joseph, the first hero in Matthew's story of Christmas, welcomed it in a way that provides a powerful example for leaders. Joseph's principles shine through in his response. Although for him, Christmas began with a great disappointment, Matthew declares that Joseph was a good man. Great leaders take their stand first as good men and women. No one becomes a leader of the highest level without developing great character. As a good man, Joseph sought to protect Mary from the consequences of what seemed like a grave moral error. Great leaders sometimes take the onus on themselves to protect good people from the worst consequences of their errors.

Joseph gave Mary's problem careful thought. Great leaders take time to think through situations involving moral dilemmas, and their character pushes them from thinking to dreaming. The rational mind can take us only so far, but greatness requires a two-sided brain that allows for creativity and revelation. As deliberation gave way to inspiration, Joseph did not fear to take on a promising project that implied personal risk. He obeyed the vision, though it entailed delayed gratification on his part. No leader gets far without accepting sacrifice as the leading edge of great reward. Finally, Joseph named the son "Savior"—declaring his faith in the success of the project. Great leaders go first in communicating to their organizations the benefits that sacrifice will bring.

Matthew certainly never thought of twenty-first-century leaders when he described Joseph's response to Christmas. But in telling the story, he gave us all a classic case study in what great leaders do every day. I hope Christian leaders today will always hit the bar that Joseph ben David of Nazareth established.

*Father of all leadership, teach us to lead our lives in such a way that the people around us are blessed, protected, inspired, honored, and saved. Give us favor with our families to inspire their trust. Let us not deny our leadership but recognize that you have called us to influence others in the advancement of your kingly will. Amen.*

*December 6*

# NO ROOM

While they were there, the time came for the
baby to be born, and she gave birth to her
firstborn, a son. She wrapped him in cloths and
placed him in a manger, because there was no
guest room available for them.
—*Luke 2:6–7*

The King James Version of the Bible renders the final
words of this verse as "no room for them in the inn."
Not only was there no room for them in the inn, there
wasn't even an inn. At least Luke doesn't mention an inn
in the original Greek version. Of course, the fictional inn
gave birth to the legend of the cruel innkeeper, who, had
he been a gentleman or had he perhaps wished to impress
the fictional hotel chain management, would have given
up his own room for a pregnant woman rather than send
her off to the stable (probably located in a cave).

More adequate, recent translations like the New
International Version or the New Living Translation

clarify that there was no "guest room" or "lodging" available for the holy family.

The scandal of this verse goes far beyond an icy-hearted innkeeper. In the culture of biblical Israel, hospitality ranked as one of the highest values. In Luke 11:5–8, Jesus tells the parable of a man who receives a surprise visit from a friend and scandalously leaves him knocking at the door until he realizes the importunate man will wake up the whole family unless the householder gets up and feeds him. Right alongside the requirement that pastors must be able to teach, Paul insists they must also be hospitable (1 Timothy 3:2). Hebrews 13:2 urges Christians to show hospitality to strangers, lest they inadvertently fail to show hospitality to angels.

Because hotels were not widely available in ancient times, travelers desperately needed protection from strangers at night. The people of Bethlehem knew well their moral responsibility. But the true scandal of the first Christmas is that there was not a single family in the town willing to make room in their house for the birth of Christ. Had they done so, we would still celebrate them to this day among the greatest heroes of Christmas.

In fact, every householder in Bethlehem became the inhospitable innkeeper. But the specter of scandal still haunts our houses today. Have we seen Jesus as a hungry, naked, thirsty, sick, or as an imprisoned stranger? Has he simply not appeared, or have we failed to see him? How will we minister to the needs of Jesus this Christmas or throughout next year?

*Lord Jesus, we would love to believe that had we lived in Bethlehem, we would have given up our rooms to receive you. Help us recognize opportunities to show our love for you in addressing the needs of innocent others who present themselves to us in your stead. Amen.*

# PRINCE OF PEACE

For to us a child is born, to us a son is given,
and the government will be on his shoulders.
And he will be called … Prince of Peace …
from that time on and forever.
—*Isaiah 9:6–7*

*A*mericans who lived during the twentieth century will never forget that December 7 is "a day that will live in infamy." On that day in 1941, the attack on Pearl Harbor made it certain that America would enter World War II. That Christmas, millions of Americans prayed to the Prince of Peace for a rapid end to the war, and indeed, to all wars.

But wars did not cease. During my youth, our people were horrified by the vivid daily images on television of the ravages of war on our own soldiers and upon the people of Vietnam. One of the most iconic images of that war captured the agony of a little girl who ran naked and burning from her village after a napalm attack by the South Vietnamese army. For my generation, no picture more graphically portrayed the horrible evil of war and its toll on the innocent.

The girl, Kim Phuc Phan Thi, tells her story in the *Wall Street Journal* and in her book *Fire Road: The Napalm Girl's Journey through the Horrors of War to Faith, Forgiveness, and Peace*:

> Forty-five years later I am still receiving treatment for the burns … But even worse than the physical pain was the emotional and spiritual pain. For years I bore the crippling weight of anger, bitterness and resentment toward those who caused my suffering. Yet … those bombs led me to Jesus Christ.[2]

Kim found her way to Jesus in 1982 through the preaching of a Vietnamese pastor, Ho Hieu Ha. He explained that Christmas was not about the gifts we give each other, but rather, about God's gift to us in Jesus Christ. She saw in Jesus the answer to the hatred and bitterness she had experienced, and walked up the aisle of the small church to say yes to Jesus. "Looking back," she said, "I understand the path I had been racing along led me straight to God."[3]

Tears filled my eyes when I read Kim's testimony of

God's power to overcome the inhumanity of war in the hearts of its victims. The day Kim ran away from the napalm would not be the defining day of her soul.

The fall of humanity indeed brought a darkness to God's creation, but another day will come in which the Prince of Peace will finally govern, and "in his name all oppression shall cease."[4]

*O Prince of Peace, guide us through this long day of infamy and sin as we run from evil. The war our enemy wages against us wreaks havoc on us and around us. Help us run along the path that will lead us straight to you. Amen.*

# GLORY AND PEACE

Suddenly, the angel was joined by a vast host
of others—the armies of heaven—praising God
and saying, "Glory to God in highest heaven,
and peace on earth to those with whom
God is pleased."

*—Luke 2:13–14 NLT*

The angels who announced the birth of Jesus declared
two things to celebrate their good news: glory (*doxa*)
to God and peace to men of good pleasure (*eudokia*).
As a good look at the Greek words suggest, doxa and
eudokia come from the same root word. Thinking about
their relationship makes the angelic gospel clearer. Both
words come from the root idea of "opinion." According to
Gerhard Kittel, "Glory (doxa) denotes that which makes
God impressive" or causes people to have a good opinion
of God.[5] The fact that the Messiah has come causes the

citizens of "highest heaven" to glorify God because they admire what God has done.

The same announcement that declared glory to God pronounced, literally, "peace on earth to people of good pleasure." To whom, exactly, does that peace belong? Modern Bible translations differ on how exactly to render the angelic phrase "of good pleasure (eudokia)." Interestingly, Luke uses another form of the same word in Luke 3:22 where God says, "You are my beloved Son; in you I am well-pleased (eudokēsa)." Who are the people, like Jesus, "on whom God's favor rests"?

One way of understanding the angelic message would be that God's favor or "good pleasure" now rested on all people because of the Messiah's birth, but that interpretation fits neither the theology of the Gospel of Luke nor the realities of the human race into which Jesus was born.

Answering the question calls on us to consider the context of the declaration. To whom did the angels make the announcement? God would soon be well pleased with the shepherds because of their response to the heralds. They hurried off to find Mary and Joseph and the baby, and after they saw the very things the angels had told of, they "spread the word" to the amazement of others (Luke 2:16–19).

God takes good pleasure in those who (1) believe the message of the gospel, (2) experience the reality of Christ in their own lives, and (3) spread the gospel to others.

As the shepherds did those things, peace came into their hearts, just as the angels had said. As a result, they joined in with the angelic army and the highest heaven, "*glorifying* and praising God for all they had heard and seen" (Luke 2:20, emphasis added).

*O God of heaven, who saints and angels adore, we pray that your declaration of peace might rest upon us this Christmas. May we rejoice at the message of the Messiah's birth, experiencing in our lives the truth of his coming. May we faithfully share with others the joy and peace we have gained, and may highest heaven give glory to you because of your favor upon us. Amen.*

*December 9*

# WORTHY WITNESSES

So [the shepherds] hurried off and found Mary
and Joseph, and the baby, who was lying in the
manger. When they had seen him, they spread
the word concerning what had been told them
about this child, and all who heard it were amazed
at what the shepherds said to them. But Mary
treasured up all these things and pondered them
in her heart. The shepherds returned, glorifying
and praising God for all the things they had heard
and seen, which were just as they had been told.

—*Luke 2:16–20*

We often hear it said that, in New Testament times,
shepherds suffered a poor reputation among Jews,
who did not accept their testimonies as valid in court.
Some writers have claimed that this fact bolsters the credibility of the Christmas accounts because no one would
have made up the idea of despised shepherds as the first
witnesses of the birth of Christ. Some Jewish literature

after the time of the New Testament does cast a shadow on the reputation of shepherds, but Professor David Croteau explodes completely the myth that shepherds lacked credibility.[6]

We read in the book of Exodus that Egyptians didn't like shepherds, but Israelites certainly did. Abraham and all the patriarchs gained their wealth as shepherds. David, the progenitor of the Jewish royal family, served as a shepherd at the time God sent Samuel to anoint him as king. Psalm 95:7 likens God to a shepherd, since "we are the people of his pasture and the sheep of his hand" (KJV). Jesus refers to himself as "the good shepherd" (John 10:11), and church leaders have borne the title of "pastor" (shepherd) since the early church (Ephesians 4:11). So much for the idea that first-century Jews saw shepherds as unreliable!

In fact, the shepherds who received the message of Christmas from the mouths of angels visited the Christ child, proving for themselves the truth of the message and serving as worthy witnesses, telling everyone exactly what they had seen and heard.

Many Christians fall into the trap of believing they lack the skills to be effective evangelists. They may feel unworthy to serve as witnesses because of their lack of eloquence or a sense of guilt over their past or even current sins. In fact, they are just as worthy as the shepherds were. The effectiveness of our witness has little to do with our worthiness. If we only let worthy people tell the Christian story, it would never get told! We should never accept the anti-witness of "the accuser of our brothers and sisters" (Revelation 12:10).

People believe the gospel because the Holy Spirit draws them to Christ. Unworthy witnesses have a role: They tell what they have seen and heard—the good things God has done for them—and the Holy Spirit makes them credible. It's not about us; it's about Jesus.

*O Father and Source of all good news, as we have sung for ages, help us go and tell it on the mountain that Jesus Christ is born. Let the Holy Spirit anoint our testimony and our declaration that we might work together with you for the salvation of the world. Amen.*

*December 10*

# THE FORERUNNER

But the angel said to him: "Do not be afraid,
Zechariah; your prayer has been heard. Your wife
Elizabeth will bear you a son, and you are to call
him John. … And he will go on before the Lord, in
the spirit and power of Elijah, to turn the hearts of
the parents to their children and the disobedient
to the wisdom of the righteous—to make ready
a people prepared for the Lord."
—*Luke 1:13, 17*

In the first few verses of his Gospel, Luke cites the final
verses of the Old Testament, in which God promised
to send the prophet Elijah before the "great and dreadful Day of the Lord" (Malachi 4:5). All three Synoptic
Gospels present John the Baptist as a resolution to that
four-hundred-year-old cliffhanger, and all four Gospels
recognize him as the forerunner prophesied by Isaiah,
who would be a voice crying in the wilderness, "Prepare
the way of the Lord."

Before John the Baptist was even conceived, an angel appeared to Zechariah to let him know that John would "go before the Lord, in the spirit and power of Elijah." Such a destiny would have an amazing effect on a young boy, who would grow up expecting his life to bring about the day of the Lord. Raised under the conditions of Nazirite vows, John would enter his ministry as a holy man expecting cataclysmic results for the unholy. His message would be one of impending judgment. To the crowds who came to him for baptism, he would cry, "You brood of snakes! Who warned you to flee the coming wrath? … The ax of God's judgment is poised, ready to sever the roots of the trees. Yes, every tree that does not produce good fruit will be chopped down and thrown into the fire." (Luke 3:7, 9 NLT).

What a surprise the ministry of Jesus would turn out to be for John. Sitting in prison, awaiting impending death, he heard about how Jesus was healing the sick and casting out demons and preaching the good news to sinners. Where was the ax? John's faith began to flag. He had faithfully executed his prophetic charge but had not expected the day of the Lord's judgment to be so long in coming. God's time is not our time.

While the "great and dreadful Day of the LORD" will indeed come, the birth of Jesus brought about a different day, one that Paul called "Today … the day of salvation" (2 Corinthians 6:2 NLT). In the Christ child, God began to show the true depths of his mercy and love to all of human-ity. Everyone who recognizes this long day of salvation will have no fear of that other day that God has mercifully delayed so that salvation may flourish among us.

*Father of all times, we recognize in this season that today is our day, the day of our salvation. Thank you for the greatness of your mercy toward us. We know that the day of the Lord will come, when Jesus will fully reign on earth and everything wrong will be set right, and we welcome it. Come soon, Lord Jesus! But while it is still today, help us spread your grace in the power of your Spirit. Amen.*

# SO MUCH GREATER

John announced: "Someone is coming soon who is greater than I am—so much greater that I'm not even worthy to stoop down like a slave and untie the straps of his sandals. I baptize you with water, but he will baptize you with the Holy Spirit!"

—*Mark 1:7–8 NLT*

All four Gospels record John's message that Jesus would baptize in the Holy Spirit. While John did not understand everything about that declaration, it nevertheless stands as the most important thing he could announce.

Baptism in the Spirit was the distinctive element of Jesus' ministry. While any holy person can baptize sinners in water to seal their act of repentance, only Jesus can baptize in the Holy Spirit. His title, Messiah, means "anointed one," as does the Greek translation, Christ.

His virgin birth—vehicle of the incarnation of God in human flesh—meant that he would be born full of the Holy Spirit. Everything he did, he did in the power of the Spirit and with the direction of the Father. Because he was anointed with the Spirit without limits, he poured out the Holy Spirit on everyone he touched. When he preached the gospel, forgave sins, healed the sick, and cast out evil spirits, he was working in the power of the Holy Spirit. After his ascension, he endued his disciples with power, baptizing them in the Holy Spirit, who would not only be with them, but also in them as the Counselor. When he comes again, he will pour out the Spirit as John expected, and all evil will come under judgment.

The ministry of Jesus carried a totally different effect than the ministry of John did. While John could lead people to repent, he could not effect the new birth in them. No righteous act could do that. "[God] saved us, not because of righteous things we had done, but because of his mercy. He saved us through the washing of rebirth and renewal by the Holy Spirit, whom he poured out on us generously through Jesus Christ our Savior" (Titus 3:5–6).

By the indwelling of the Holy Spirit poured out on us by Jesus, we can live new lives infused with the presence and direction and power of God. John was the greatest of the biblical prophets, but he could never do that, and that's what makes Jesus so much greater!

*Baptize us, Lord Jesus Christ, with your Spirit this Christmas. Let us lean in to God's indwelling power in us. Forgive, deliver, heal, and empower us. In this season, do miracles among us according to our faith and fullness in you. Let all the saints live up to the power that dwells within us. Amen.*

# A BIGGER PICTURE

He is the image of the invisible God, the firstborn
of all creation. For by him all things were created, in
heaven and on earth, visible and invisible, whether
thrones or dominions or rulers or authorities—all
things were created through him and for him. And he
is before all things, and in him all things hold together.
And he is the head of the body, the church. He is
the beginning, the firstborn from the dead, that in
everything he might be preeminent. For in him all the
fullness of God was pleased to dwell, and through him
to reconcile to himself all things, whether on earth or
in heaven, making peace by the blood of his cross.

—*Colossians 1:15–20 ESV*

At Christmas, we usually think of the baby Jesus—a
sweet, tender image that only begins to reveal his
identity. When I was a student in college, I liked a Christian
bluegrass group called the Zion Mountain Folk. They
played a terrific ballad called "Bigger Picture of Jesus."[7] We

need a bigger picture because we so often base our concept of Jesus on ourselves or other people we have known. In reality, he transcends any human who has ever lived.

The writings of Paul never discuss the birth of Jesus in Bethlehem, focusing instead on his status as "the *firstborn* of all creation." The historic creeds of Christianity clarify that Jesus was "begotten, not made," and Paul declares that his status places him before all created things. He is also "the *firstborn* from the dead," who attained resurrection into a body that transcends our moribund fleshly existence and guarantees eternal life to all who follow him—the maker of the New Creation and the second Adam in it.

The picture gets bigger and bigger the more you look at it. Jesus is the visible image of the invisible God! The fullness of God lived in him, so he stands preeminent over everyone ever born of woman.

If we only think of Jesus as Mary's firstborn son, we miss the bigger picture.

*Holy Jesus, we recognize today that you are God. Thank you for joining us in our humble estate, for suffering all things that we suffer, sharing every aspect of our pain and struggle and joy. Thank you for feeling what we feel, knowing what we know, and going where we could not go to do what we could never do. In you we are reconciled to God. Amen.*

*December 13*

# CHRISTMAS FOOD

He has filled the hungry with good things but has
sent the rich away empty.
—*Luke 1:53*

C hristmas, one of the great feasts of the church, has
been celebrated for many centuries with the prepa-
ration and sharing of food. Some see it as the best meal of
the year, although some Americans see the Thanksgiving
feast as the best. At Christmas potlucks in businesses and
churches and homes around the country, people bring
their favorite dishes to share.

Strangely, it seems that the biblical stories relating to
Christmas do not record that anyone brought food to the
holy family or anyone else, despite the comical assurances
of no less an authority than Garrison Keillor that the
word *myrrh* in fact referred to a Mediterranean hot dish.[8]
But in fact, someone did bring food at the first Christmas.

In the Magnificat, Mary's hymn of exultation about

God's miraculous act of filling her womb, she says, "He has filled the hungry with good things but has sent the rich away empty." At the first Christmas, God provided the food. It might be objected that Mary exulted in God's historical acts of salvation for his people, such as the provision of manna and quail to the Israelites in the dessert. But I believe she made an argument that God's action in begetting a messianic son through her constitutes a culmination and recapitulation of all God had done before.

In sending his Son, God truly brought us food. Born in a manger—a feeding trough—Jesus referred to himself as food on multiple occasions. After he fed the 5,000, Jesus declared, "I am the bread of life. Whoever comes to me will never go hungry, and whoever believes in me will never be thirsty" (John 6:35). On that same occasion, he said, "Very truly I tell you, unless you eat the flesh of the Son of Man and drink his blood, you have no life in you. Whoever eats my flesh and drinks my blood has eternal life, and I will raise them up at the last day. For my flesh is real food and my blood is real drink. … This is the bread that came down from heaven. Your ancestors ate manna and died, but whoever feeds on this bread will live forever" (John 6:53–55, 58). Jesus recognized that the gift of his life was a recapitulation and a culmination of the giving of manna in the wilderness.

The Lord's Supper follows up on this great truth and enjoins us to celebrate the feast regularly in remembrance of him and as prologue to the great marriage supper of the Lamb, which he will eat with us at the end of history. This Christmas, let us celebrate the feast in the knowledge that God has given us true food and true drink in the person of Jesus.

*"The eyes of all," O Lord, "wait upon thee, and thou givest them their meat in due season." Thank you for the delightful foods we will eat this Christmas, but greater thanks we offer for the truth that we do not live by bread alone but by the Word that abides forever with us. Amen.*

*December 14*

# CHRISTMAS MYTHS

So reprimand them sternly to make them strong
in the faith. They must stop listening to Jewish
myths and the commands of people who have
turned away from the truth. Everything is pure to
those whose hearts are pure.
—*Titus 1:13–15 NLT*

In the twentieth century, many Jews arrived in America as immigrants and refugees, determined to make a place for themselves in the land of the free and contribute to the well-being of the country. In assimilating into American culture, they needed to figure out whether or how to celebrate Christmas. Unsurprisingly, artists took the lead. Christmas was too American to ignore, and asserting their Jewishness in the entertainment industry had only limited appeal. So instead of insisting that people not wish them Merry Christmas or sitting out the holiday in sullen resentment, they invented a new set of Christmas traditions based on winter and snow and Santa Claus and created new Christmas myths that would not be threatening to the religious or non-religious sentiments of non-Christians.

They wrote monster hit songs like "Winter Wonderland," "Have Yourself a Merry Little Christmas," "White Christmas," "It's the Most Wonderful Time of the Year," "Let It Snow," "I'll Be Home for Christmas," "Sleigh Ride," "Chestnuts Roasting on an Open Fire," "Silver Bells," and "Santa Claus Is Coming to Town." They created new myths like Rudolph the Red-Nosed Reindeer and Frosty the Snowman.[9] All in all, they created a secular way to celebrate Christmas.

So what should a Christian's response look like? Paul offers a key: "Everything is pure to those whose hearts are pure." As Christians, we should be well aware of our indebtedness to Jews for everything they have contributed to our lives. Celebrating winter and snow and sleigh bells and family certainly count as purehearted things. Charming moral stories like Frosty and Rudolph do no harm. Unlike Titus' Cretans of old who were taking religious myths seriously, no one takes the children's myths of Christmas seriously.

Christian leaders since the first century have recognized that followers of Jesus have no choice but to participate in the cultures they live in. While evil must be rejected, harmless things can be enjoyed. Ensuring that Jesus receives honor at Christmas does not depend on whether the entertainment industry or secular people celebrate the birth of Jesus or remain silent at Christmas. It depends upon Christians showering their neighbors with love and friendship so that everyone knows and enjoys our observation of the real reason for the season.

*O Father of our Lord and Savior, season our lives with love and grace so that as we celebrate Jesus this year at Christmas, we should be worthy to be seen as the sweetest and most affectionate of people. Let all sour attitudes fall away, all rivalries cease, all bitterness fade. Make us living testimonies of the love for all people that moved you to send Christ into the world. Amen.*

*December 15*

# SANTA CLAUS

> In the same way, some think one day is more
> holy than another day, while others think every
> day is alike. You should each be fully convinced
> that whichever day you choose is acceptable.
> Those who worship the Lord on a special
> day do it to honor him.
> —*Romans 14:5–6 NLT*

One of my favorite Christian leaders, Dr. George O.
Wood, loves to tell the story of a church where a
man stood up during the service at Christmastime and
delivered a stern "prophetic word" against Santa Claus. A
kindly soul in the church immediately stood and coun-
tered, "Thus saith the Lord: Lay off Santa Claus. He's a
good brother, and he's doing a good work." The story has
been told so many times that it brings a hearty chuckle in
some circles to commend someone by saying, "You're a
good brother, and you're doing a good work."

So what should we make of Santa Claus? As history records, the goodly Nicholas of Myra, a saintly bishop of the fourth century, saw so many miraculous answers to prayer that he became known as Nicholas the Wonder-worker. After his death, it didn't take long for the miracle stories to go ballistic, suffering increasing exaggeration to the point that he became the mythical Santa Claus we celebrate today—able to descend tall chimneys in a single bound, circumnavigate the whole world within a few hours, and deliver billions of presents to the delight of us all.

Like the Christmas myths we considered yesterday, Santa Claus is as American as apple pie. We celebrate him in good fun. No one worships Santa Claus or prays to him or confuses him with Jesus. Dueling prophecies do seem to be a bit much. The "prophet" who commended dear Santa probably did so to make sure no children present would feel dismay over the condemnation of their beloved Kris Kringle. (I'm a bit of a believer, as I met the official Santa Claus at a church in North Pole, Alaska and visited him at the Santa Claus House there. He had a real, long, white beard and was indeed a dear brother in Christ. I have a picture with him.)

My parents played the Santa Claus game with me as a child, and we let our children enjoy the game as well. Because we explained it all to them at the proper age and clearly differentiated between the silly story of Santa and the precious truth of Christmas, their faith in Jesus suffered no lapse when they found out that we pretended to believe in Santa just for fun. To the purehearted, everything is pure.

Our concern at Christmas should not be that people might have too much fun. Neither should we feel jealousy on Jesus' behalf if people do not pay enough attention to the manger. Rather, we should either join in the fun as purehearted people or decline to play the Santa game with a good spirit and full conviction of faith in Christ. In either case, we should take special care to do everything in honor of the Lord, making sure that Jesus reigns in our families and our hearts as the true star of Christmas and that the joy he brought to earth is reflected in our own faces.

*Creator of good humor and source of all true fun, we thank you for all the joys and pleasures we experience at Christmas. As we open presents this year with people we love, may our joy please you. May our good cheer reflect your eternal confidence in the outcome of your plan for creation and redemption. Be honored in our hearts and in our homes. Amen.*

December 16

# COMMERCIALISM

"The merchants of the earth will weep and mourn
… because no one buys their cargoes anymore."

—*Revelation 18:11*

"There's a lot of bad 'isms' floatin' around this world," said Alfred, the Macy's janitor in the classic Christmas movie *Miracle on 34th Street*, "but one of the worst is commercialism. Make a buck, make a buck. Even in Brooklyn it's the same—don't care what Christmas stands for, just make a buck, make a buck."[10] Apparently, Alfred hadn't thought about Stalinism and other "bad isms" that were beginning to burst onto the scene. But it has become a nostrum to complain at Christmastime about the meaning of Christmas being lost amidst the hustle and bustle of shopping.

I gained a new perspective on all this years ago while serving as a missionary overseas. While I was driving home around midnight from the airport in mid-December, freezing rain fell as temperatures dropped into the thirties in the high altitudes. I stopped at a traffic light, and trembling children approached my car, wet, cold, and hungry, their adult handlers standing just across the way. (They were not alone. Across the city, thousands of poverty-stricken people from the countryside had surged in to beg for charity at Christmas.) As I bought their flowers and then gave them back, hoping they could sell them again, I rejected the spiritualization of poverty.

I see the flurry of buying and selling at Christmas as a beautiful thing. Many stores operate all year long at a loss until the Christmas season pulls them solidly into the black. Accordingly, millions of employees and their families prosper all year long because of Christmas. I see no dishonor to Christ at all in the giving of gifts to our families, friends, and charities around Christmas, but I have seen shame frozen on the faces of parents around the world, whose hungry children were begging at Christmas because their national economy could not generate enough honest work to create a prosperous society.

Of course, anything that becomes an "ism" can become a false religion, and the book of Revelation depicts the final end of idolatrous commercialism. We must never let commercialism be the meaning of our Christmas celebration, nor let idolatry tempt us to borrow money we have no means to repay just so we can buy more dazzling gifts.

My favorite Christmas occurred during those missionary years. We were struggling economically, the cost of our international move having seriously depleted our funds. We had almost no money to celebrate Christmas, but we decorated a tree, and my wife Kathleen stretched our funds to make sure our two towheaded treasures would have toys under the tree. When it came time for my little girls to give me a gift, they giggled with excitement over what they had bought, and their beauty exceeded description. I still count the gold-filled cuff links they gave me that year among my favorite possessions—not because of their minimal commercial value but because of the priceless joy they bring to mind.

*Father, we recognize that every good and perfect gift comes from above, descending from the Father of lights. May we never exalt worldly prosperity to heaven's place in our hierarchy of values, but trust in you for the provision of all we need on earth and in heaven. Amen.*

# REJOICE!

## FEAST OF LAZARUS

When he had said this, Jesus called in a loud voice,
"Lazarus, come out!" The dead man came out, his
hands and feet wrapped with strips of linen, and a
cloth around his face. Jesus said to them, "Take off
the grave clothes and let him go."
—*John 11:43–44*

The church's tradition calls for Christians to rejoice
on the third Sunday of the Advent season (Gaudete
Sunday) in anticipation of Christmas but also in celebration of Lazarus, whom Jesus raised from the grave. I have
always found it interesting that we know almost nothing
about Lazarus. We know he lived in Bethany, had two sisters, died, and came out of the tomb at the command of
Jesus. We don't know what he did afterward.

So why did Jesus raise him from the dead? Often,
when someone narrowly escapes death or recovers from

what people expected to be a mortal illness, we will assume that God must have spared them for some reason, perhaps so they could accomplish some great task. But it doesn't necessarily work that way. Jesus said the death and resurrection of Lazarus occurred "so that you may believe. But let us go to him." The ever-gloomy Thomas replied, "Let us also go, that we may die with him" (John 11:15–16).

A few highly unreliable oral traditions arose over the centuries that followed. According to one of them, Lazarus came back so traumatized by what he had seen during half a week in hell that he never smiled again, despite living an additional thirty years. Such a story may have served to scare medieval people so they would want to avoid hell—though even modern folks should seek to avoid hell—but it serves better to tell us what not to do with the eternal life we have received. We should not live out the rest of our lives in gloom waiting for heaven.

Eternal life, as the Gospel of John presents it, does not refer to something we have to wait for. Rather, it's the quality of life (literally, the life of the ages or of the world to come) we begin to live when we come to faith in Christ. Those who know by faith that they have inherited eternal life, beginning now, have every reason to rejoice greatly!

God has a place for everyone, and we all know and love a person with an "Eeyore personality." As the story of Lazarus suggests, the apostle Thomas does seem to have had a naturally melancholic disposition. John the Baptist, whom we also celebrate in the third week of Advent, also seems to have had less than a sunny mien. We don't have to go around in a fake happy state—even at Christmastime. But every one of us should shake off the blues from time to time and recognize that Christmas means joy to the world. Especially for those who have put their faith in Jesus and begun to live in the age to come.

*O Holy Spirit and Giver of Life, anoint us today with the oil of joy, as the Father anointed Jesus. Help us fix our attention on the truth that Christ has defeated death—not only for Lazarus but also for everyone who trusts in him. Like the disciples who saw Lazarus come forth, we know that Christ has risen—once and for all! We lift up our hearts unto you, rejoicing evermore, praying continually, giving thanks in everything, and fulfilling the will of God in Christ Jesus. Amen.*

# MELANCHOLY CHRISTMAS

He has brought down rulers from their thrones,
but has lifted up the humble.
—*Luke 1:52*

One of my favorite Yuletide songs is "Christmas Time Is Here." Written by Lee Mendelson and Vince Guaraldi for the 1965 TV special *A Charlie Brown Christmas*, it combines a melancholy jazz tone with happy lyrics.[11] As I was thinking about why I like the song so much, I wondered why I should feel melancholy at Christmastime, the time for "tidings of great joy" (Luke 2:10 KJV). It immediately occurred to me that as the solstice approaches, the year and the sunlight gradually die out, and at the age of fifty-eight, nothing about shorter days seems cheerful to me. But my sense of melancholy at Christmas goes beyond the mere calendar.

I also considered that Christmas present always

reminds me of Christmas past. I remember particular Christmas mornings of my childhood and gifts I received with excitement, but I also remember the dark years of my teens when my mother decided to stop decorating our home for Christmas and got rid of the Christmas tree and other "pagan" trappings. I remember the sadness that accompanied her descent into depression, then divorce, and I remember the first Christmas after she left, when I rebelled against the gloom and went out into the woods to cut down a juniper tree and lead my family in a return to decorating and celebrating Christmas.

When Kathleen and I established our home, we started an annual tradition of buying or making a special ornament to remind us of the best thing that happened to us each year. Every Christmas we rehearse the story of God's grace in our family over the years. Along with all of the best memories, I always think about the struggles we've overcome each year.

But amidst all of the loosely bridled joy at Christmas, melancholy finds its root in the Christmas event itself. Christians have a long tradition of singing melancholy songs, such as "O Come, O Come Emmanuel" and "What Child Is This?" and other songs in minor keys. Christmas may have meant joy to the world, but it meant awe, reflection, and pain for Mary and Joseph. It meant humility and weakness and vulnerability for the baby Jesus, and a life of human struggle.

So amidst the joy that came to the world, a bit of sober melancholy can do us some good, as giddiness and awe and silliness and wonder and shallowness and depth all come together at one time in the same place for the same reason. It's right to embrace seriousness at Christmas, and also to celebrate with great joy. As you observe the holidays this year, may the presence of God go with you.

*O Man of Sorrows, crucified for our joy, we embrace you in gratitude. Surely you bore our sorrows, and by your stripes we were healed. Forgive us our sins, as we forgive those who have sinned against us. Help us in our seriousness to keep your joy in mind. Amen.*

# CHRISTMAS HUMILITY

And Mary said: "My soul glorifies the Lord and my spirit rejoices in God my Savior, for he has been mindful of the humble state of his servant. From now on all generations will call me blessed, for the Mighty One has done great things for me—holy is his name."
*—Luke 1:46–49*

Corazón Aquino took over an impossible situation when she was elected president of the Philippines in 1986, and she handled it with a humility that astounded the world. Her strength, serenity, honesty, and integrity became an example to all nations. When she accepted the prestigious Fulbright Award after her term ended with a peaceful transfer of power to an elected successor, she said:

It all began with an ordinary person, placed by Providence at the head of quite ordinary people like herself. I am not a hero like Mandela. The best description for me might, after all, be that of my critics who said: She is just a plain housewife.[12]

Being humble doesn't mean you can't do great things! Mary displayed the same kind of humility when she agreed to serve God as the virgin mother of the Messiah. She realized that she had no claim to deserve her election. She was just an ordinary person. But she knew that God could use her humble state. In the Magnificat, her song of praise to God, she identified herself with the poor and those needing mercy, the humble and the hungry. When Jesus named the community of the blessed in his Sermon on the Mount, he could have addressed those beatitudes directly to his mother. And like those Jesus saw as blessed, Mary recognized that all generations would call her blessed.

James 4:6 and 1 Peter 5:5 declare that "God opposes the proud but gives grace to the humble" (NLT). In her humility, Mary received grace to conceive and give birth to Jesus, and to raise him in godliness. If we aspire to do great things for God, we would do well to model ourselves on the humility of Mary and allow God to conceive within us a vision we could never dream up on our own. Humility will empower us with grace, but pride will bring God's opposition.

We thank you, Lord Jesus, for becoming meek and lowly for us, and for the power you modeled from below. Help us see ourselves as we truly are, and never estimate our future on what we are today, but grow daily in the power of trust in you. Amen.

*December 20*

# SILENT NIGHT

## VIGIL OF THOMAS

> The time came for her baby to be born. She gave
> birth to her firstborn son. She wrapped him
> snugly in strips of cloth and laid him in a manger,
> because there was no lodging available for them.
> That night there were shepherds staying in the
> fields nearby, guarding their flocks of sheep.
> —*Luke 2:6–8 NLT*

On this night, the church has observed the Vigil of Thomas, and it provides an interesting occasion for thinking about the watchful night that Mary and Joseph and the shepherds spent long ago in Bethlehem. Many Christmas carols celebrate that night, from the bombastic "O Holy Night" (in which singers try to wake up the angels *in excelsis* with its climactic high note) to the sentimental "Away in a Manger" (in which, "the little Lord Jesus, no crying he makes." As Thomas might have concluded, this is doubtful).

Perhaps two Austrians provided the world's favorite carol about Bethlehem: "Silent Night." In 1818, a pastor named Joseph Franz Mohr convinced a composer friend, Franz Xavier Gruber, to set his poem to music in a rush so that his church choir could use it later that night in his midnight Christmas Eve mass. As the Salzach River had flooded the church, disabling the pipe organ, the piece had to be written for guitar accompaniment. The choir and the guitarist quickly learned the piece, and the rest is history. Tradition in Austria calls for abstaining from singing "*Stille Nacht*" until Christmas Eve.[13]

We have no reason to think that the Bethlehem vigil actually passed by any more quietly than any other night. Occasioned by the loud proclamations of herald angel hosts, interrupted by inevitable baby cries, punctuated by late lowing or early crowing and the din of crickets, the night likely brought little silence. Luke's account tells us of the amazement of the shepherds and the fact that they immediately begin to tell everyone what they had seen—perhaps even waking neighbors to do so.

Yet the song convinces us because it serves as an icon. Unlike an idol, which a worshiper looks to, one looks *through* an icon. When we look at reality through the lens of the Bethlehem vigil, we see heavenly peace. We feel the quiet in our souls, and we project it upon that faraway, long-ago, holy night. Like Mary, we ponder what we have seen and heard and treasure it in our hearts.

*Lord Jesus, no longer a baby but forever one of us, we thank you for peace. Thank you for every silent night we spend in peaceful sleep, but also for your presence in the midst of turmoil and trouble. Make us aware of your presence, no matter what we may face. Amen.*

# CHRISTMAS AND DOUBT

## FEAST OF THOMAS

> When Joseph woke up, he did what the angel
> of the Lord had commanded him and took
> Mary home as his wife.
> —*Matthew 1:24*

Christians for many centuries have celebrated the Feast of Thomas on this day, which usually coincides with the winter solstice. The coincidence was surely no accident, as the sun shines least on this darkest day of the year and many people struggle with seasonal affective disorder during this time, experiencing depression and melancholy. Thomas, as we remember, was the melancholy disciple who, among other things, doubted the Lord's resurrection.

Christmas can be a time of doubting as well as a firm

affirmation of faith. Some doubt that Christmas should be celebrated at all. In fact, the first Christmas didn't occur in winter, as shepherds did not usually tend their sheep at night in the open fields during winter. Clement of Alexandria recognized around AD 200 that estimates of Christ's birthday varied widely, with all convinced it occurred in the spring or summer. Still, a couple of centuries later, Augustine confidently averred that Jesus "was born on the day which is the shortest in our earthly reckoning and from which subsequent days begin to increase in length."[14] Augustine had accepted a popular theory that Jesus had died on March 25 and that he must have been conceived on the same day, making December 25 his birthday—a date coinciding with the winter solstice on the Roman calendar.[15] I definitely doubt they were correct.

Others may doubt the Christmas miracle itself—that "the Word became flesh and made his dwelling among us" (John 1:14). The Gospels of Matthew and Luke declare virgin birth as the means by which God begat a Son in the person of Jesus. Though such a miracle clearly would pose no challenge to the God who made humanity from the dust of the earth, many have found the virgin birth difficult to believe—especially in the short, dreary days of mid-December when the whole world seems darkest.

But consider Joseph. Angelic visitation or not, he must have suffered doubts. Had an angel from the Lord really visited him, or could it have been an evil spirit? Had Mary suffered a moral lapse before he could take her into his home? Could he manage the social shame that would follow him when people began to realize that he "must have" succumbed to temptation before his marriage was finalized?

No miracle can compel so thoroughly that we cannot doubt it when the mind suffers from mental illness or emotional wounds or fatigue or trial beyond its strength. But Joseph believed God, acted on his belief, and faithfully protected the blessed virgin who bore his Savior and ours. Who are we to let doubt win when he held on to faith so steadfastly?

*O Father, who has given us your only begotten Son so that believing on him we may have eternal life, lift our hearts in these dreary days of winter; renew our hope; delight our souls; and strengthen our faith to do good works for your glory as the whole world joins us in the celebration of Jesus. May our efforts inspire others to believe in the miracle of Christmas. Amen.*

# CHRISTMAS ANGELS

It was revealed to [the prophets] that they
were not serving themselves but you, when they
spoke of the things that have now been told you
by those who have preached the gospel to you
by the Holy Spirit sent from heaven. Even
angels long to look into these things.
—*1 Peter 1:12*

Just as men and women throughout the centuries of
the Old Testament pondered the messianic prophecies to try to discern the plan of God and the times of
its fulfillment, the angels wondered when the time would
come. Angels do not enjoy omniscience, and just as they
did not know when the Messiah would come, they do not
know the day nor the hour of Christ's return (Matthew
24:36). But like Anna and Simeon, who frequented the
temple in anticipation of the consolation of Israel (Luke
2), the angels longed for the day to come.

When the time had fully come, we see the thickest

flurry of angelic activity in all the Bible. Angels appear to Zechariah, Joseph, Mary, and the Galilean shepherds to announce the forerunner, the conception, and birth of the Messiah. Throughout the ministry of Jesus, the angels stood by, waiting to be dispatched into service. Every twist in the plot amazed and delighted them. They appeared after the resurrection, rolling away the stone and declaring the good news to the women who followed Jesus. After the ascension, they announced that Jesus would return in the same way in which he had ascended.

But they don't know when he will return. They long to look into these things and to receive the day of God's victory, but like us, they have to wait. They will get the announcement of God's unfolding plan just before we do, and they will spring into action with alacrity, to do what angels do—declare the message!

Until then, they still do God's work among us. We never know when we may encounter an angel, and Hebrews 13:2 says that some people have entertained angels without knowing it. Acts 13:7–15 reflects the ancient Jewish belief that we all have a guardian angel that watches over us. We will probably never see an angel, but one thing seems certain—they serve with an eager expectation of the coming of Christ.

As we speak and sing of angels at Christmas, we should not train our eyes to perceive them in our midst, but rather, like them, fix our eyes on Jesus, longing for the day of his appearing.

*O God who rules in heaven, who has made us a little lower than the angels and makes servants flames of fire, anoint us with the oil of gladness as we remember the birth of our Savior and look forward to the next advent of our Lord. May our longing for your presence in heaven light our path through this dark world. Like the angels of Christmas, may we announce your gospel to everyone, especially during this most wonderful time of the year. Amen.*

# HOME
# FOR CHRISTMAS

She gave birth to her firstborn son. She
wrapped him snugly in strips of cloth and
laid him in a manger, because there was no
lodging available for them.
—*Luke 2:7 NLT*

s the old song made popular by Bing Crosby says, everyone dreams about being home for Christmas, with snow and presents and mistletoe.[16] It's a beautiful idea. And in American culture, we associate no time of the year more with home and family than Christmas.

Everyone wants to be around that Christmas tree or seated at the Christmas dinner table, enjoying the family circle in warmth and safety. But when you think about the first Christmas, none of the heroes were home for the occasion. Mary and Joseph had left home—they couldn't even find a guestroom. The shepherds had left their fields and flocks. The wise men had traveled far, far from home on the road to see the Christ child sometime after Christmas. Jesus, of course, went the farthest from home—leaving the glory of heaven and the fellowship of the Father and the Spirit to take on the humility of human birth. As a matter of fact, only the villains of the Christmas story—Herod and the infamous imaginary innkeeper (and all the real, inhospitable householders of Bethlehem)—were at home. In a great irony, the true meaning of Christmas has nothing to do with being at home. It has everything to do with leaving home on a noble and holy mission to save those who have become lost and helpless without God, who face the danger of losing their heavenly home for eternity.

I'm so glad Jesus left home to save us and that the heroes of Christmas left home to be with him and attend his humble birth. I'm thankful for members of the military who spend Christmas away from home in defense of our nation and its values. I'm also thankful for the missionaries who will spend Christmas away from home this year in gospel service around the word. Like the heroes of Christmas, they have left home to attend the new birth of others.

*O God, we pray that you will visit everyone who spends this Christmas away from home in service to others and that the true Spirit of Christmas— God's Holy Spirit—will anoint their efforts and multiply the gifts of God in their lives so that they may present to God the souls of thousands when we all finally do get home, once and for all. Amen.*

*December 24*

# SALVATION THROUGH CHILDBIRTH

## FEAST OF ADAM AND EVE

> Then the LORD God said to the serpent … "I will
> cause hostility between you and the woman, and
> between your offspring and her offspring. He will
> strike your head, and you will strike his heel."
> —*Genesis 3:14–15 NLT*

On the surface, God's cursing of the serpent seems pretty straightforward and simple. Snakes and humans generally hate each other and, in the wild, will usually attack each other at first threat. On a spiritual level, the curse might be understood to imply that Eve would gain victory over her enemy by having children, who would ensure human survival and continue the battle against our enemy. But Christians have perceived a "prophetic surplus" in the meaning of these words ever since Mary's offspring crushed the "serpent" that struck him. The Son of Man, born as a second Adam from a virgin's womb, would provide the ultimate victory over Satan.

Satan hates God and knows he has no ability to win a war against heaven. God's vast power has already defeated and displaced him, but he rages on in exile, carrying out a proxy war against God's beloved humanity, since war on God will always prove futile. Having fallen into sin, humanity must choose to renounce the devil and his works and, seeming to have no power of our own to defeat him, rely faithfully on God's help. Still, Paul suggests that humans have a surefire way of defeating Satan—the bearing of children.

God has eternally willed to bring many sons and daughters to salvation, and God takes special delight in every human baby that enters the world. Satan, on the other hand, hates human children and wills to destroy each and every one of them. In our age, abortion and rampant voluntary infertility subvert the survival of peoples, as low birth rates ravage the populations of the developed nations. Satan is pleased and humanity suffers defeat.

The battle is dangerous indeed. As Luther wrote and taught us to sing, "His craft and power are great, and armed with cruel hate. ... Our striving would be losing were not the right Man on our side, the Man of God's own choosing."[17]

Childbirth has kept humanity flourishing since the beginning, but it would have all been for naught without God's Chosen Son. Had Mary not borne the Son of Man—the offspring of a virgin's womb who would win the decisive battle over Satan at the cross—our defeat would have been certain. Imagine Satan's glee as the nails bit into and through the heels of Jesus on the cross; imagine his consternation when Christ stood on those same heels in triumph over death, hell, and the grave! Jesus' triumph was the ultimate fulfillment of an oh-so-subtle prophecy of human victory over our enemy.

*O holy Child of Bethlehem descend to us, we pray; cast out our sin, and enter in, be born in us today. Let us walk in the victory that you have provided through your life, death, and resurrection. Protect us in the spiritual battle that rages around us and extend your saving grace over all the world. Help us defeat sin and evil on every hand. Bless every pregnant woman with a sense of the saving dignity she represents. Give us another generation, born into our world, that we may make glad the heart of God. Amen.*

December 25

# TODAY I HAVE
# BEGOTTEN YOU

## FIRST DAY OF CHRISTMAS

> I will proclaim the LORD's decree: He said
> to me, "You are my son; today I have become
> your father. Ask me, and I will make the
> nations your inheritance, the ends of
> the earth your possession."
>
> —Psalm 2:7–8

As we saw in Isaiah 9, the royal psalms of the Davidic dynasty, composed for use in the coronation of Israel's kings, set the tone for the messianic prophecies that would be fulfilled in Jesus. In all the pomp and ceremony of the coronation, Israelites, like other peoples of antiquity, symbolically viewed the kings as having been born again as sons of God. The first day of their reign was, in a way, the day they truly began to live.

When Mary bore Jesus in Bethlehem, the royal psalms took on a much more literal fulfillment. The very Son of God appeared in human flesh. As God's own creative act made Adam, Christ became a second Adam placed in a virgin's womb. While no Israelite king ever literally received the nations as his inheritance, Jesus had earned the sovereign right to rule all nations by his death on the cross for every man and woman on earth. In his future capital, the New Jerusalem, every nation, people, tongue, and tribe will one day parade before his throne declaring, "Salvation belongs to our God … and to the Lamb" (Revelation 7:10). "The kingdom of the world has become the kingdom of our Lord and of his Messiah, and he will reign for ever and ever" (Revelation 11:15).

As we celebrate the birth of Christ, we do so as those who have joined in his reign. Part of our celebration of his birth springs from our own adoption as sons and daughters of God. Born again by the Spirit who overshadowed the Virgin Mary, we have passed from death to newness of life. Because of Jesus' birth, death, and resurrection, we ourselves have been born of God.

People say that everyone turns back into a child at Christmas. Perhaps that blessed childlike nostalgia comes from our recognition that we celebrate not only the birth of Jesus but our own royal birth and coronation as well. Who doesn't feel like a child on their birthday? Merry Christmas to you!

*O Lord and Father of all, we come to you with jubilant thanksgiving. We cast our victors' crowns before you, recognizing that all glory belongs to Christ. We yearn for the day of his coming, when his glory will be revealed in us, when the children of God will be revealed. Though we know not what we will be, we know that we will be like him and will see him as he is. By that light, we will penetrate all darkness, enduring the bondage of time, until he comes to reign. Amen.*

*December 26*

# THE FEAST OF STEPHEN

## SECOND DAY OF CHRISTMAS

When the members of the Sanhedrin heard this,
they were furious and gnashed their teeth at him.
But Stephen, full of the Holy Spirit, looked up to
heaven. … "Look," he said, "I see heaven open and
the Son of Man standing at the right hand of God."
—*Acts 7:54–56*

As a great traditional carol teaches,

*Old King Wenceslaus looked out*
*on the feast of Stephen,*
*when the snow lay round about*
*deep and crisp and even.*
*Brightly shone the moon that night,*
*though the frost was cruel,*
*when a poor man came in sight,*
*gath'ring winter fuel.*

Moved by the man's need, Wenceslaus said to his page,

*Bring me flesh and bring me wine.*
*Bring me pine logs hither.*
*Thou and I will see him dine*
*when we bear them thither.*[18]

In England, people traditionally celebrate the Feast of Stephen as Boxing Day, an occasion that calls on the wealthy to serve the poor. Bosses give "Christmas boxes" to their employees—just as King Wenceslaus did. Consider in the light of such a tradition the death of Stephen, the church's first martyr. He gave his life to publicly declare that Jesus was the Son of Man, whom prophets had announced long before. In declaring Jesus as God in human flesh and blood, he offered the flesh that was truly food and the wine that was truly drink. His hope was to feed the bread of eternal life to the leaders of his people, but the powerful turned on him and stoned him to death instead.

And so, ironically, on the Feast of Stephen, tradition calls Christians to seek out those who are less wealthy and less powerful than themselves and feed them. Some day this week would be a wonderful day to serve the poor at a rescue mission in your city, or perhaps to send an offering to your favorite Christian relief and development ministry.

The point, in the end, is not to honor Stephen but to follow the example of the One who left the privileges of heaven to enter our poor world with the bread of life, Jesus.

*O great Giver of Life, we thank you for all of the blessings we have received this year and for the food we have eaten with joy this season. May we never dine to excess, forgetting or ignoring the hungry, lest Jesus should pass us by incognito. Receive our generosity to meet their needs as a gift offered unto the Lord Jesus himself. Amen.*

# THE BELOVED DISCIPLE

## THIRD DAY OF CHRISTMAS

Near the cross of Jesus stood his mother, his
mother's sister, Mary the wife of Clopas, and Mary
Magdalene. When Jesus saw his mother there, and
the disciple whom he loved standing nearby, he
said to her, "Woman, here is your son," and to the
disciple, "Here is your mother." From that time on,
this disciple took her into his home.
—*John 19:25–27*

The Feast of St. John celebrates the disciple Jesus loved.
The Gospel of John mentions Jesus' love for all of his
disciples (13:1) and for Mary, Martha, and Lazarus (11:5).
Before he died, Jesus said, "Greater love has no one than
this: to lay down one's life for one's friends" (15:13). Out
of humility, the author refers to himself as the beloved
disciple, aware that all of the disciples could say the same.

When Mary visited the temple to consecrate Jesus,

Simeon had told her "a sword will pierce your own soul" (Luke 2:35). When the soldier at the cross thrust his sword into Jesus' side, Mary's own soul bled. Jesus, who loved his mother, made sure that someone would be at her side when that moment came, delegating the care of her to John, his best friend.

John's consciousness of Jesus' love determined the course of his future. The new commandment Jesus gave, "Love one another. As I have loved you, so you must love one another" (John 13:34), became the central feature of John's apostolate. It resounds over and over again in his Gospel and his letters. Tradition tells us that even as an old man in his nineties, John continued to travel to the churches with one message: "Love one another."

No message can better express the meaning of Christmas. As John 3:16 recorded, "God so loved the world that he gave his one and only Son, that whoever believes in him shall not perish but have eternal life." In perfect coordination, 1 John 3:16 says, "This is how we know what love is: Jesus Christ laid down his life for us. And we ought to lay down our lives for our brothers and sisters." 1 John 4:11 says, "Dear friends, since God so loved us, we also ought to love one another."

On this third day of Christmas, we still have plenty of time to make our love known to our family and friends, our brothers and sisters in Christ, and others who stand outside the circle of faith and family.

*O Triune God, who from all eternity has lived in the loving fellowship of the Father, the Son, and the Holy Spirit, we thank you for being the author and source of all love. As you have loved us, help us love those we live with—giving ourselves in sacrificial service for their good. May everyone in our family feel our love this season. May our neighbors and coworkers and even our enemies see in us the reflection of your holy love. Amen.*

# THE HOLY INNOCENTS

## FOURTH DAY OF CHRISTMAS

When Herod realized that he had been outwitted
by the Magi, he was furious, and he gave orders to
kill all the boys in Bethlehem and its vicinity who
were two years old and under, in accordance with
the time he had learned from the Magi.
—*Matthew 2:16*

The book of Revelation confirms that Jesus is "the
Lamb who was slain from the creation of the world"
(13:8). God's decision to create humanity with free will
meant that necessarily, we would need a Savior, and the
destiny of Jesus was set along with ours. Nothing could
have stopped his sacrificial death for us.

On the other hand, the baby boys of Bethlehem,
known in church tradition as the Holy Innocents, died
needlessly. They had no part in God's plan of salvation.
They were not unavoidable "collateral damage" in the war

for our souls. Rather, they died because of the savage cruelty of one man. Herod would insist to the very day of his death that no one would ever oust him, even putting members of his own family to death to ensure that they could never unseat him from his throne.

How we might wish that Herod were a singular case! Yet many people of comparable cruelty have ruled over nations and peoples throughout our history. Stalin, Hitler, Pol Pot, and Saddam Hussein number just a few of the mass assassins of our own time, and their type litters and profanes human history. All of them insisted that they would rule over others, killing the innocent to maintain their wicked grasp on power, right up to the day of their deaths.

These monsters are not "Everymen." They stand out among the worst of us. But the individual autonomy they lived and killed for threatens to spoil the lives of us all. Will we rule our own lives as petty kings and queens (whether as undeniably wicked or seemingly innocuous), or will we surrender to the kingdom of God that Jesus brought to our world? Will we rule our own lives or let King Jesus reign in us?

Perhaps one in a billion among us will become a Herod, but the truth remains: If we hold on to the rule of our life, there will be casualties all around us. Who will we hurt by holding on to the power to rule our lives? Will it be a betrayed spouse? An unborn child (tragically, the world's largest group of holy innocents)? A neglected son or daughter? A broken friendship? A trampled coworker? Will the people around us who deserve our love and service become the "holy innocents" in our story? Or will we ourselves be the gravest victims of our own willful refusal to surrender to the Lord of all?

The deaths of the Holy Innocents in ancient Bethlehem serve to remind us that something real is at stake in our lives. Will we be part of God's kingly campaign or wage our own futile battle for control?

*O King of the universe, you who know me by name and gave your only Child for me, I surrender the lordship of my life to Christ that he may increase and I may decrease. Let your will be done on earth—in me—as it is in heaven. By your Spirit, teach me to consider others before myself, to give up my own privileges to bless and empower them, to lead only as it may serve them, to flourish only as it may increase the prosperity of others. Rule and reign over and through me forever. Amen.*

# STAR OF BETHLEHEM

## FIFTH DAY OF CHRISTMAS

> After Jesus was born in Bethlehem in Judea, …
> Magi from the east came to Jerusalem and asked,
> "Where is the one who has been born king of the
> Jews? We saw his star when it rose and have come
> to worship him." … After they had heard the king,
> they went on their way, and the star they had seen
> when it rose went ahead of them until it stopped
> over the place where the child was. When they
> saw the star, they were overjoyed. On coming to
> the house, they saw the child with his mother
> Mary, and they bowed down and worshiped him.
> —*Matthew 2:1–2, 9–11*

The church calendar recognizes today as the Feast of King David, the original "star" of Bethlehem. In modern times, the hexagram or "Star of David" has come to symbolize the Jewish people, but the Bible never associates David with a star. Nevertheless, the famous star recorded in Matthew's Gospel welcomed the birth of David's messianic descendant.

The Old Testament clearly condemns astrology, which has nothing to do with biblical revelation. But God led the magi to Bethlehem through a unique combination of their astrological analysis and his divine direction. Nothing in their art could have pointed them to a particular house in Bethlehem! But God mysteriously and specifically indicated exactly where they would find the Christ child. In a mathematical analogy, the magi arrived at the right answer, in spite of using a flawed method.

In fact, there is no wrong way to find Jesus. I have often said, "There are bad reasons to come to Christ but no bad reasons to stay with him." Some people go looking for Jesus because they fear hell or because they believe that Christ will return at any moment. Others fall in love with a Christian and start going to church. I've seen people start going to church because they wanted to play on a church-league softball team. Once they get to church, they find Jesus, and in the end, nothing matters more than that! Once we find him, we begin to realize how little we understood before we sought him.

The best reason to crown Jesus as King recognizes his incomparable worth. We should serve Christ because he deserves all honor, glory, power, and dominion. The fact that we start with our own needs should bring no shame. No matter how we got to Jesus, the greatness of his love and presence offers all the reason we'll ever need to follow him.

*Holy Lord, you are the only Star we will ever worship. May we be deeply aware of your worthiness and love you for your own sake. Hallowed be your name in the world, worshiped in every nation, and especially by me and mine. Amen.*

# HEIR OF ALL THINGS

## SIXTH DAY OF CHRISTMAS

In the past God spoke to our ancestors through
the prophets at many times and in various ways,
but in these last days he has spoken to us by his
Son, whom he appointed heir of all things,
and through whom also he made the universe.
The Son is the radiance of God's glory and the
exact representation of his being, sustaining
all things by his powerful word.

*—Hebrews 1:1–3*

The book of Hebrews presents the richest language in the
New Testament, and it starts with a big bang! Through
the Word, God created the universe, but during the second
creation, the Word was born! God *spoke* the final, defini-
tive word of prophecy that would declare the whole divine
nature and plan to humanity. In Jesus, God said it all.

The Christology of the book of Hebrews soars to
the highest place. Jesus is shown to have been coeternal

with the Father, active with him in creation, sustaining everything in the force that set it all in motion—his own powerful Word.

The high Christology of Colossians 1 and Hebrews 1 forms the scriptural basis for orthodox doctrine. While no one understands the full nature of the Trinity, Hebrews 1:3 speaks about Christ as the "radiance of God's glory and exact representation of God's being." We might think of creation as the mirror in which that radiance and representation can be seen. Not only does the creation allow God's glory to shine for men and angels to see, but it also allows us the incredible glory of participation in the reflection.

As the Son of God who participated integrally in the creation, Jesus therefore stands as the "heir of all things" (Hebrews 1:2 KJV). The crown jewels are the nations of the world (Psalm 2:8). Before Jesus, every knee will bow and every tongue will confess that he is King of Kings and Lord of Lords.

*Heir of all things, we thank you that through you, we too are heirs of God and coheirs, if indeed we share in your sufferings. Help us persevere in faithfulness to you and the good works God has predestined us to fulfill, in order that we may also share in your glory. Amen.*

*December 31*

# COME, LORD!

## SEVENTH DAY OF CHRISTMAS

He who is the faithful witness to all these
things says, "Yes, I am coming soon!" Amen!
Come, Lord Jesus!
—*Revelation 22:20 NLT*

When I was seven years old, Israel fought a six-day war against Arab powers led by Egypt, Syria, and Jordan. The war began on Monday and raged through the week. On Thursday, my friend Doug, who attended the Baptist church at the end of our street, told me that he had heard at church that Jesus was going to return on Saturday. I followed the news on Thursday and Friday as Israel pushed into the territories of its enemies and victory became imminent. By Saturday—Sunday in Israel—the war was won.

It seemed perfectly reasonable to me that Jesus would come on Saturday, just as my friend had warned, and sure enough, as I played in the street in front of my house that afternoon, a rushing, mighty wind blew down our street with a cloud of dust. I was a skinny, little guy, and the gale-force gust literally knocked me off my feet. I thought I was being whipped up in the rapture but quickly realized I was going down, not up. In a panic—it all happened in the twinkling of a dusty eye—I reached out for something to hold onto, grabbing the radio antenna of my dad's green 1962 Pontiac Catalina and snapping it off. I fell, only minimally impeded, onto the street.

Looking around, I saw no one. I was all alone. Obviously, I had not been found worthy to be caught up into the air with Jesus and the saints of all ages. Perhaps it had been the doubt I had expressed in reaching for the antenna that had frustrated the blessed hope for me. Since I saw no friendly faces around, I assumed that trouble would be coming, and I ran and hid—you're not going to believe this one—in a wooden coffin crate my dad had gotten from my uncle Jerry, an undertaker.

Consigned to my sepulchral refuge, I waited and waited. It seemed an eternity but probably lasted only five minutes or so in real time. I finally crawled out of the sarcophagus and turned to face "what rough beast might come slouching toward [Demopolis, Alabama] to be born."[19] Relieved to find my parents and family still at home, I immediately knew the Lord had not come, and I did not have to worry whether I had been left behind.

Over the years to come, I would wonder several times, upon entering an empty house after school, whether I had missed the rapture, each time committing myself to greater holiness so as to be ready on the day of Christ's appearing. As a result of these experiences, I developed a certain "apocalypse fatigue." Never again will anyone get me very alarmed about the idea that particular world events spell an immediate return of Christ. On the other hand, my determination to be ready and joyful about the prospect of Christ's return has left me always hoping, as Andraé Crouch used to sing, "it won't be long." As we observe the beginning of a new year, the idea that Jesus could return this year should bring our fondest, most passionate hope. Come, Lord, this year!

*Come, Lord Jesus! Let our greatest resolution today be that you will find us watching for you when you return. Amen.*

*January 1*

# THE YEAR
# OF FAVOR

## EIGHTH DAY OF CHRISTMAS

You are observing special days and months and
seasons and years! I fear for you, that somehow I
have wasted my efforts on you.
—*Galatians 4:10–11*

Despite the Christian tradition of special holidays,
the New Testament sometimes frowns on the
celebration of special days. In Galatians, Paul says that
by returning to a ceremonial, calendrical religion, the
Galatians had returned either to pagan bondage or to ser-
vitude under the Jewish law. Christianity, Paul explains,
has nothing to do with the formal recognition of special
dates, but rather with celebrating life in the Spirit every
day. Paul asked, "Having begun in the Spirit, are ye now
made perfect by the flesh?" (Galatians 3:3 KJV).

How can we celebrate the new year in a truly Christian way? Jesus celebrated, symbolically, a new year in Luke 4:18–19:

"The Spirit of the Lord is on me, because he has anointed me to proclaim good news to the poor. He has sent me to proclaim freedom for the prisoners and recovery of sight for the blind, to set the oppressed free, to proclaim the year of the Lord's favor."

Looking up from the scroll, he pronounced, "Today this scripture is fulfilled in your hearing" (v. 21). Not only did he declare a new year, "the year of the Lord's favor," he declared a whole new age—the age of the Spirit. For those in Christ, every year lived in the fullness of the Spirit counts as the year of our Lord. Every day offers a holy day for the saints of God.

So have we been celebrating these special holidays in vain? Not if we have done it while living in the Spirit! As Paul himself said, "There is now no condemnation for those who are in Christ Jesus, because through Christ Jesus the law of the Spirit who gives life has set you free from the law of sin and death" (Romans 8:1–2).

*O Ancient of Days, we recognize that every day is today for you, and that your love for us never varies. But as we declare this new year to be the year of our Lord, may we see your favor as never before. Let others recognize your favor in our lives, and let no effort to bless us be wasted. Keep our eyes on you, not the calendar, until the day when all time shall cease. Amen.*

*January 2*

# THE CONSECRATION

## NINTH DAY OF CHRISTMAS

When the time came for the purification rites
required by the Law of Moses, Joseph and Mary
took [Jesus] to Jerusalem to present him to the
Lord (as it is written in the Law of the Lord,
"Every firstborn male is to be consecrated to the
Lord"), and to offer a sacrifice in keeping with
what is said in the Law of the Lord: "a pair of
doves or two young pigeons."
—*Luke 2:22–24*

In bringing the baby Jesus to the temple, Mary and
Joseph participated in a very religious act, carefully
obeying the law of Moses. It is often said in our times that
Christianity is not a religion; it's a relationship. Such a slo-
gan misses the whole point of religion. Perhaps a more
accurate but less pithy statement would be that Christianity is not a matter of empty religious rites; rather, it is

heartfelt religious practice in a personal relationship with God. In any case, whatever we do to pursue our personal relationship with God unavoidably becomes a form of religious practice.

If we genuinely claim to follow Jesus, we will commit ourselves to practicing religion, just as he did. Mary and Joseph were *tzadekim*—righteous Jews who walked faithfully in the law of Moses. Jesus himself practiced Judaism, living in obedience to the law at the deepest level. When he went to John the Baptist to receive his baptism, he did it "to fulfill all righteousness" (Matthew 3:15). Like Jesus, true Christians are religious people. They pray, they fast, they attend religious services, they read the Bible, they get baptized and participate in Holy Communion, they marry their spouses, they consecrate their children to the Lord, and they celebrate feasts like Christmas and Easter. And they do it with all their hearts—not out of some sense of obligation but because practicing Christian religion gives them a closer personal relationship with God.

Slogans have a role. They reduce complex ideas into highly simplified, pithy statements. They often produce a bit of shock and provoke deeper thought. But if they fail to stimulate more careful thinking, they can mire a person in shallowness. Empty religious rites can do the same thing. The answer for all of us requires us to constantly invest deep and innovative thinking, sincere and fervent emotion, and consistent and disciplined religious practice in our relationship with God.

Like Jesus did.

*O God, whose Word is living and active, let us never fall into lifeless religion, but may we experience frequent revival. As in any human relationship, our sense of connection to you waxes and wanes. During this Christmas season, let us truly consecrate ourselves to you. Draw us closer. Speak to us. By the indwelling Spirit of Christ, be Immanuel, God with us. Amen.*

# THE CONSOLATION

## TENTH DAY OF CHRISTMAS

> Now there was a man in Jerusalem called Simeon,
> who was righteous and devout. He was waiting
> for the consolation of Israel, and the Holy Spirit
> was on him. It had been revealed to him by the
> Holy Spirit that he would not die before he had
> seen the Lord's Messiah. Moved by the Spirit, he
> went into the temple courts. When the parents
> brought in the child Jesus to do for him what
> the custom of the Law required, Simeon took him
> in his arms and praised God, saying: "Sovereign
> Lord, as you have promised, you may now
> dismiss your servant in peace."
> —*Luke 2:25–29*

The birth of Jesus came at a very low ebb in the
life of the Jewish people. After losing their sovereignty when the Davidic dynasty was overthrown, they

suffered captivity in Babylon, Greek imperialism and the desecration of the temple, exile throughout the world, domination and military occupation by the Romans, and the humiliating and brutal rule of Herod, an Edomite (Idumean). They longed for consolation, the fulfillment of Isaiah's prophecy:

> "Comfort, comfort my people," says your God. "Speak tenderly to Jerusalem. Tell her that her sad days are gone and her sins are pardoned. Yes, the LORD has punished her twice over for all her sins." (Isaiah 40:1–2 NLT)

Israel had suffered for so long, but Simeon faithfully believed God's word to him that he would live to see Israel's consolation through the long-awaited rule of the Messiah. Once he had seen the baby Jesus, he knew he could die in peace.

The kingdom of God that Jesus preached truly brought consolation to everyone who entered in, but it did not bring an end to Roman oppression, nor to the dominion of empires over Jews and other oppressed peoples of the world. That day will come, but the peace Simeon received by faith suffices for those who trust in Jesus. We have already begun to live the life of the age to come, and so we live in patient hope for the consummation of all things.

I remember the faith my grandparents lived out

with respect to the Lord's return. They lived every day in ardent hope for the rapture of the church as Paul taught in 1 Thessalonians 4:16–17: "For the Lord himself will come down from heaven. ... First, the believers who have died will rise from their graves. Then, together with them, we who are still alive and remain on the earth will be caught up in the clouds to meet the Lord in the air" (NLT). Like Simeon, my grandparents thought they would never taste death before the coming of the Lord. When he came for them early, they were not disappointed. I want to live in the same hope and expectation.

*Hasten the day of your coming, Lord. As we celebrate your birth, we cannot avoid thinking of the day of your return, when you will establish the reign of God over all things and will be exalted before all people. We long to be gathered together with you and with the saints who have gone before us. Until then, let us live in ardent hope, in deep consolation, and in the full conviction of eternal life. Amen.*

*January 4*

# O Little Town

## Eleventh Day of Christmas

> When [King Herod] had called together all the
> people's chief priests and teachers of the law, he
> asked them where the Messiah was to be born. "In
> Bethlehem in Judea," they replied, "for this is what
> the prophet has written: 'But you, Bethlehem, in
> the land of Judah, are by no means least among
> the rulers of Judah; for out of you will come a
> ruler who will shepherd my people Israel.'"
>
> —*Matthew 2:4–6*

Small towns have always suffered from feelings of inferiority. The Old Testament prophet Micah spoke directly to the little town of Bethlehem, assuring it that its small size would not keep it from great glory. Just as David, the ruler of Israel's golden age, and his illustrious ancestors Boaz and Ruth had come from Bethlehem, the future scion of David and Savior of Israel would also come from Bethlehem.

I was born and grew up in the small town of Demopolis, Alabama. As a child, I felt very provincial and wondered if I could compete with people from large cities—the people I saw in movies and television programs who lived such extravagant lifestyles with unimaginable, seemingly limitless wealth and sophistication. One of my school teachers falsely told me that while we Southerners played wind instruments in bands, Northern children played stringed instruments in orchestras and could identify the composers of classical music pieces by just listening to a few bars. I definitely felt inferior but also challenged to compete!

Young people from small towns often respond competitively to the challenges of their humble origins. But neither the limitations of small-town origins nor the competitiveness they may inspire have anything to do with the rise of Jesus to the highest place, for he was given "the name that is above every name, that at the name of Jesus every knee should bow" (Philippians 2:9–10). What catapulted Jesus to fame and then to glory was the destiny that God had decreed for his life and his faithful obedience to God's plan.

God has destined each of us for glory and declared it in prophecy. In Romans 8:18–19, Paul reckons that "our present sufferings are not worth comparing with the glory that will be revealed in us. For the creation waits in eager expectation for the children of God to be revealed."

Small-town origins present the least of a person's impediments to glory. Suffering, setbacks, sins, and sorrows all beset us. But "to those who by persistence in doing good seek glory, honor and immortality, [God] will give eternal life" (Romans 2:7).

Knowing that God has destined us for great things should motivate us all to persist in seeking God's best, no matter what origins or obstacles we may face.

*In the name of the Father and the Son and the Holy Spirit, we pray that we might fix our eyes on Jesus, the pioneer and perfecter of faith, who for the joy set before him endured the cross, scorning its shame, and sat down at the right hand of the throne of God. May we never fall over the stumbling blocks of this world but persist unto life everlasting. Amen.*

*January 5*

# EXILE—THE PATH TO POWER

## TWELFTH DAY OF CHRISTMAS

After the wise men were gone, an angel of the
Lord appeared to Joseph in a dream. "Get up!
Flee to Egypt with the child and his mother," the
angel said. "Stay there until I tell you to return,
because Herod is going to search for the child
to kill him." That night Joseph left for Egypt with
the child and Mary, his mother, and they stayed
there until Herod's death. This fulfilled what the
Lord had spoken through the prophet:
"I called my Son out of Egypt."
—*Matthew 2:13–15 NLT*

During my years as an expatriate living in a certain
country, several national leaders fled the country to avoid imprisonment. Once when I lamented the

departure of one of them, a friend said to me, "Don't worry about him. In our country, you can't rise to the presidency unless you have first spent time as a political exile." The status of exile can serve as proof of the dramatic patriotism that maximum leadership demands.

Nevertheless, political exile constitutes a grave offense against human rights. Article 19 of the Universal Declaration of Human Rights insists that "everyone has the right to freedom of opinion and expression; this right includes freedom to hold opinions without interference." Article 14 also states that "everyone has the right to seek and to enjoy in other countries asylum from persecution."[20]

As the Roman Catholic papal encyclical *Exsul Familia Nazarethana* says:

> Jesus, Mary and Joseph, living in exile in Egypt to escape the fury of an evil king, are, for all times and all places, the models and protectors of every migrant, alien and refugee of whatever kind who, whether compelled by fear of persecution or by want, is forced to leave his native land, his beloved parents and relatives, his close friends, and to seek a foreign soil.[21]

According to Matthew 25:40, when we serve such people, we minister to Jesus in the same way.

The exile to Egypt did not represent the first time Jesus would abandon his rights for our well-being. Before emptying himself of his human rights, Jesus had put aside his divine rights by taking human form (Philippians 2:7). And the flight to Egypt wasn't the last time he would suspend his human rights for us, but rather, it was the first instance in a long series of ironies. In the end, his exile from heaven and the sacrifice of his human rights made possible the inexorable day of his coronation as King for life over all humanity. And his life and reign will be eternal.

*Holy Lord, God of power and all authority, as we face setbacks and contradictions in this world, let us not lose sight of your sovereignty and the fact that you will give us justice in due season. Let us care more about our duty to serve than our right to be served. Be our defender and shield. Amen.*

*January 6*

# SHINING LIKE
# A STAR

## EPIPHANY

Some wise men from eastern lands arrived in
Jerusalem, asking, "Where is the newborn king of
the Jews? We saw his star as it rose, and we have
come to worship him." … When they saw the star,
they were filled with joy! They entered the house
and saw the child with his mother, Mary, and
they bowed down and worshiped him. Then they
opened their treasure chests and gave him gifts
of gold, frankincense, and myrrh. When it was
time to leave, they returned to their own country
by another route, for God had warned them in a
dream not to return to Herod.

—*Matthew 2:1–2, 10–12 NLT*

The wise men who visited the manger where Jesus
lay came as pilgrims. Although their faith in astrology would never have helped them understand the full

significance of the star, God recognized the sincerity of their faith and revealed to them that the birth of the King of the Jews carried both cosmic and personal significance. They had to go west in order to get orientation for their lives. Deciding to offer their worship to the divine child, they began their journey westward, navigating by faith the whole way. Like Abraham of old, they did not know where they were going. They confronted doubts, dangers, challenges, and sacrifices. But in the end, they went back to their country richly rewarded, sharing their pilgrim tales from the very cradle of salvation.

Many travelers find Jesus in the midst of their journey. Perhaps an economic motive drives them. Maybe they travel for adventure. Some of them search for something indefinable. But God knows the reasons that put them on the road to the Savior. Without their knowing it, God guides them until they find Jesus and offer him their worship and their treasures.

Such people, upon their return to their place of origin, no longer travel as tourists or wanderers or migrant workers. The have been converted into accidental pilgrims. They didn't know that their divine destiny would carry them to the knowledge of God. They never suspected that they would return to their country as missionaries. For the rest of their lives, they will share the story of how the Lord led them to the cradle of salvation in a distant land.

*Lord of our calling, we pray today, in memory of the magi, that you would bless those who travel today. No matter the motive for their movement, we ask that they would arrive at their own epiphany, coming to the knowledge of God in Christ today. As we travel this year, make us mindful that others on the road are lost and in need, and that we should point them toward Jesus. Make each of us like a star, shining in a dark and perverse world, so that on the day of Christ we will not have traveled in vain. Amen.*

*Epilogue*

# CHRISTMASTIME ALL YEAR THROUGH

As this book illustrates, I love Christmas. I never get tired of celebrating it, and in fact, I believe that celebrating Christmas every day is the secret to living a Spirit-filled life. The phrase "Spirit of Christmas" may conjure for some a Dickensian ghost from Christmas Future or Christmas Past, but the true Spirit of Christmas is none other than the very Spirit of God.

The Holy Spirit overshadowed the Virgin Mary to make the first Christmas real (Luke 1:35). By the Spirit, Zechariah spoke the first public prophecy announcing the coming of the Messiah (Luke 1:67). As a baby, John the Baptist leapt in his mother's womb, full of the Spirit before his birth (Luke 1:15). Simeon, moved by the Spirit, appeared at the temple courts to meet the newborn King and declare his coming to bring light to the nations and glory to Israel (Luke 2:25–30). Such intimate involvement in the first Christmas merited the title "Spirit of Christmas," and the Holy Spirit continues to deliver every good and perfect gift that comes from the Father.

True Christianity requires walking in the Spirit. Without that empowerment, we have nothing but empty religion. Jesus promised, near the end of his ministry, that if he went away, he would send the Comforter (John 14:16), the Holy Spirit, to take his place among us, to abide in our hearts, to give us words to proclaim the Christ. The same Spirit who conceived Christ in Mary attends our new birth, gives us words to prophesy and proclaim the Christ, and anoints us with power so that signs might reinforce our witness. The Spirit of Holiness aids us in our sanctification and inspires us to hope. Every good thing we associate with Christmas flows to us from God's Spirit.

If we think of celebrating Christmas all year through in terms of the kitschy paraphernalia of trees and tinsel and mistletoe and carols and chocolates, we miss the whole point of the occasion. Those things must be left largely in December for our own good. But the Spirit of Christmas must remain with us all year long, lest we fail to live as Christians at all. My prayer for you is that God will fill you richly with the Holy Spirit, bringing miraculous help to your everyday life throughout the year to come, and indeed, throughout your whole life.

 **Joseph Castleberry** is president of Northwest University, a Christian college in Kirkland, Washington. He and his wife, Kathleen, have three daughters: Jessica (married to Nathan Austin), Jodie (married to Roberto Valdez), and Sophie, plus two grandchildren (Emerson and Miranda), who all love to celebrate Christmas with their families. Readers are encouraged to contact Dr. Castleberry at joseph. castleberry@icloud.com.

# Notes

1   Edwin and Jennifer Woodruff Tait, "Why Do We Have Christmas Trees?" *Christianity Today*, December 2008, https://www. christianitytoday.com/history/2008/december/why-do-we -have-christmas-trees.html.

2   Kim Phuc Phan Thi, *Fire Road: The Napalm Girl's Journey through the Horrors of War to Faith, Forgiveness, and Peace* (Chicago: Tyndale Momentum, 2017); cited in "The Salvation of 'Napalm Girl,'" *Wall Street Journal,* December 21, 2017, https://www.wsj.com/articles/the-salvation-of-napalm -girl-1513899109.

3   Kim Phuc Phan Thi, *Fire Road: The Napalm Girl's Journey through the Horrors of War to Faith, Forgiveness, and Peace* (Chicago: Tyndale Momentum, 2017).

4   Adolphe Adam, "O Holy Night," 1847, https://www.hymnsand carolsofchristmas.com/Hymns_and_Carols/o_holy_night.htm.

5   G. Kittel, G. Friedrich, and G. W. Bromiley, *Theological Dictionary of the New Testament* (Grand Rapids, MI: Wm. B. Eerdmans, 1985), 178.

6   David Croteau, "Christmas Urban Legends: Shepherds As Outcasts," *Lifeway*, December 17, 2015, https://factsandtrends.net /2015/12/17/christmas-urban-legends-shepherds-as-outcasts/. See also *Urban Legends of the New Testament* (Nashville: B&H Academic, 2015).

7   Zion Mountain Folk, *Grass Roots Music*, Track 3, Light Records, 1978.

8   Garrison Keilor, *Life Among the Lutherans* (Minneapolis, MN: Augsburg Fortress, 2010), 56.

9   Rob Kapilow, "Why Many Classic Christmas Songs Were Written by Jewish Composers," *The Star,* November 30, 2017, https://www.thestar.com/news/insight/2017/11/30/why-many-classic-christmas-songs-were-written-by-jewish-composers.html.

10  *Miracle on 34th Street*, written and directed by George Seaton, 20th Century Fox, 1947.

11  Lee Mendelson and Vince Guaraldi, "Christmas Time Is Here," 1965. From *A Charlie Brown Christmas*, animated film, written by Charles M. Shultz, directed by Bill Melendez, featuring Peter Robbins, Chris Shea, Kathy Steinberg, and Bill Melendez, Lee Mendelson Films, 1965.

12  Corazón Aquino, "Speech Upon Receipt of the Fullbright Prize," Washington, DC, October 11, 1996, https://www.scribd.com/document/103656313/Speech-Upon-Receipt-of-the-Fulbright-Prize.

13  Hyde Flippo, "Stille Nacht/Silent Night—The True Story," *The German Way & More*, 2017, https://www.german-way.com/history-and-culture/holidays-and-celebrations/christmas/stille-nacht-silent-night/.

14  Andrew McGowan, "How December 25 Became Christmas," *Bible History Daily*, December 3, 2017, https://www.biblicalarchaeology.org/daily/biblical-topics/new-testament/how-december-25-became-christmas.

15  William J. Tighe, "Calculating Christmas: The Story Behind December 25," *Touchstone*, December 2003, http://touchstonemag.com/archives/article.php?id=16-10-012-v.

16  Kim Gannon and Walter Kent, "I'll Be Home for Christmas," Decca Records, 1943.

17  Martin Luther, "A Mighty Fortress Is Our God," c. 1529, https://www.hymnal.net/en/hymn/h/886.

18  John Mason Neale and Thomas Helmore, "Good King Wensaslaus," *Carols for Christmas-tide*, 1853, https://www.hymnsandcarolsofchristmas.com/Hymns_and_Carols/good_king_wenceslas.htm.

19 William Butler Yeats, "The Second Coming," in *Michael Robartes and the Dancer,* Thomas Parkinson and Anne Brannen, eds. (Ithaca, NY: Cornell University Press, 1994).

20 UN General Assembly, *Universal Declaration of Human Rights,* December 10, 1948, 217 A (III), http://www.un.org/en/universal -declaration-human-rights.

21 Pope Pius XII, *Exsul Familia Nararethana,* encyclical letter, *Papal Encyclicals Online,* August 1, 1952, http://www.papa lencyclicals.net/pius12/p12exsul.htm.

*Your Deepest Dream: Discovering God's True Vision for Your Life* (NavPress, 2013)

*The Kingdom Net: Learning to Network Like Jesus* (My Healthy Church, 2014)

*The New Pilgrims: How Immigrants Are Renewing America's Faith and Values* (Worthy, 2015)

*Los Nuevos Peregrinos: Cómo los inmigrantes están renovando la fe y los valores de los Estados Unidos* (Worthy Latino, 2015)

*Visul Inimii Tale: Descoperind adevarata viziune a lui Dumnezeu pentru viata ta* (Life Publishers, 2015)

# Notes

# Notes

# Notes

# Notes